ADVANCE PRAISE
Blacklisted from the PTA

~⚬~

"Lela Davidson's *Blacklisted from the PTA* is a hilarious and honest take on motherhood. With her laugh out loud funny writing style and her laser focus attention to detail, Davidson will crack moms up and make them say, 'Yes, that's exactly what I was thinking.' A truly entertaining novel for any exhausted mom or mom-to-be."

Kelly Wallace, Chief Correspondent, iVillage/NBC Universal

"Birth, babies, tooth-fairies, baking, junk drawers, car trouble, computer viruses, the PTA, date nights, big box stores, family travel, and girlfriend getaways—no suburban stone goes unturned in this promising debut by Lela Davidson. This collection of quickie-read essays serves up a sly look at suburban bliss. The book is in brief episodes like Carrie Bradshaw meets *Desperate Housewives*, only Davidson is anything but frantic. Instead she's sassy, smart, and seductive with her wry coverage of the middle-class trenches. Tongue in her cheek and pen in her hand, just when we all needed it most, Davidson brings family funny to the fore. Moms especially will appreciate the laughs."

Christina Katz, Author of *Writer Mama* and *The Writer's Workout*

"I so dearly loved this book. Funny, witty, insightful and the perfect read when you're hiding in a bathroom stall during a PTA meeting."

Wendi Aarons, MouthyHousewives.com

"In *Blacklisted from the PTA*, Lela Davidson strips away all the glossy perfection of motherhood and marriage as sold to us on the covers of *Parenting* and *Cosmo*. Instead Davidson gives us the true glimpse of a woman progressing through the evolving stages of her life as part of a modern family living in the burbs, and she does so with both a buoyant charm and twisted humor that keeps you giggling from cover to cover. Anyone who reads this book will wish they had Davidson as a best friend because her hilarious honesty and insights on raising children, loving her husband, and accepting middle-age make it feel safe for us to confide that we are not the flawless parent or spouse as dictated by society, but rather that we are human, and that's perfectly okay."

Ron Mattocks, Author of *Sugar Milk, What One Dad Drinks When He Can't Afford Vodka*

"Lela's essays prove to be a rewarding read from the first page to the very last. This entertaining and thoughtful collection of essays will reassure readers that, if nothing else, they are not alone in their 'unperfectness,' and that it is not only 'okay' it should be celebrated."

Kimberly Enderle, Editor-in-Chief, *Peekaboo*

"From getting busted by the cops for backyard karaoke to a top ten list for literally getting blacklisted from the PTA, Lela Davidson's collection is witty and light. Perfect for red lights."

Rita Arens, Editor of *Sleep Is for the Weak*

"Fresh, insightful, and clever! Lela Davidson never allows her writing to sink into the Hallmark cliches of what motherhood is supposed to be. Instead, she shares the brutal and hilarious truth about what it means to be a mommy in today's world. Readers will recognize their sisters, their BFFs and themselves in her witty accounts."

Kiki Bochi, Editor, *Broward Family Life*

"In *Blacklisted from the PTA*, she has succeeded in writing a universal collection of short personal stories that are shockingly honest! The fact that each story is a juicy 5 minute confession is so addicting, I'll admit I squeezed in 'just one more,' one too many times. In *Blacklisted From the PTA*, Lela Davidson presents the thoughts you think, but somehow, writing them down is pure genius…and pretty damn funny."

Christine Candelaria, Blogger and iVillage Contributor

BLACKLISTED

from the PTA

Lela Davidson

JUPITER PRESS

Blacklisted from the PTA
by Lela Davidson

ISBN: 978-1-936214-43-3

Library of Congress Control Number: 2011923314

Author Photo: Calotype-Photography.com

Published by Jupiter Press, imprint of Wyatt-MacKenzie

jupiterpress@wyattmackenzie.com

LELA DAVIDSON

For John, Alexander, and Gabriella, my daily support
and inspiration.

∽oᴥo∼

FOREWORD

by Lisa Quinn

Author of *Life's Too Short to Fold Fitted Sheets* (Chronicle Books)

～❦～

THERE IS A CERTAIN ACTRESS IN THIS MONTH'S VOGUE. SHE'S
striking a glamorous pose in her perfectly appointed Tribeca
kitchen, preparing "YUMMY!" locally grown, organic, butternut
and beeswax after school snacks in an $865 Michael Kors crepe
flounce skirt and 7-inch Louboutins. Her hair looks amazing,
her skin sun-kissed, and while there appear to be a few toys
tossed about, there is not an actual child to be found. Curious.
In the interview, the starlet suggests several times that the key
to all this happiness is finding balance.

Duh. When will women ever learn?

Is it bad that I want throw a greased watermelon at her to see
how well she maintains that balance in those platform heels?

The moment I met Lela Davidson I knew we were kindred
spirits. She lives on the perfect cul-de-sac in the perfect suburb
where the lawns are pristine and the neighbors always wave. But
here's the thing: she's no perfect mother—and proud of it. While
some moms spend entire evening tirelessly manufacturing
impressive crepe paper peonies for the bake sale centerpiece,
our gal would rather laugh than fret. She understands that a

smile on her kid's face is more important than a gold star on a chart somewhere, and if she's wearing Louboutins in the kitchen, you better believe the kids are at Grandma's and she's not making after school snacks. While her Prada bag may fake, she's the real deal. And if those women in the PTA can't handle it? Well, their loss is our gain.

The stories in this book are self-deprecating, honest, and funny. Lela Davidson opens up so we can too. You're going to love it.

INTRODUCTION

I DIDN'T PLAN TO WRITE THIS BOOK. WHAT I WANTED TO WRITE was a novel, one of those quirky romantic titles that get made into a movie starring Reese Witherspoon or Kate Winslet. I didn't know how to do that, so I set out to learn. Write what you know, the experts said. But what did I know? I knew how to quit a real job and pack up a family to move from Seattle to Texas, and that the Pampered Chef was not the vehicle to my self-actualization. All I seemed to be good at was sitting on the driveway drinking boxed Chardonnay and talking to my friends. So that's what I wrote—the stories that made us laugh. I hope they make you laugh, too.

More importantly, I hope that each and every one of you find your way to the PTA's blacklist.

TABLE OF CONTENTS

∼☙∽

Birth, Babies, and Beyond

The Terrible Twos, Give or Take a Few

Suburban Bliss

Blacklisted

Happily Ever After

The Journey

Me Time

Birth, Babies, and Beyond

Birth: You Can't Plan It

THE MORNING MY DAUGHTER WAS BORN I ROSE WITH THE SUN, listened to birds singing, and timed contractions. Then I called my doula, whose job it was to ensure that all doctors, nurses, anesthesiologists, surgeons, friends, family, and husbands, stuck to—The Birth Plan.

In case you're unfamiliar with the concept, The Birth Plan consists of detailed instructions regarding how your baby will enter the world. It is formulated in the comfort of your living room while you and your doula sip tea and admire each other's pedicures. The actual *birth* takes place in a greenish room where instead of chamomile, you would gladly accept heroin from a street dealer should one conveniently appear.

After suffering through one unplanned cesarean, I wanted to actualize my womanhood by pushing that second baby out. Most women worship the doctor who offers a scheduled C-Section. Not me; I'm special. I opted for a VBAC—vaginal birth after cesarean—and in so doing also made my choice for *minimal pharmaceutical assistance.*

"Natural childbirth was fine, Honey," my mother told me. "But that was before we had the drugs."

I told myself I didn't need the drugs. For hours I labored according to The Birth Plan. I breathed, counted, and groaned. It sucked. I got stuck in the bathtub, unwilling to move. Even when the water got cold I stayed there moaning like an injured cow. The contractions came so fast and lasted so long that they merged into one continuous, gnawing, increasingly unbearable pain.

After eight hours, the physical torture finally brought me to my senses. I agreed to take the drugs. Just a little mind you—just enough to blunt the edge. But Demerol, it turns out, is a gateway drug. Forget natural; I wanted the needle. My Grape Nut eating, placenta-planting doula was disappointed when I requested the epidural, but she supported me anyway. It was, after all, a legitimate stipulation in Plan B, paragraph 3 of The Birth Plan.

I spent the next several hours turning from side to side, elevating one or another part of my body, and visualizing my baby descending the birth canal. This is WAY easier when you're high! But my baby didn't want to come out. We would get her just to the brink and she'd twist herself back around, sunny side up. After hours of monitoring and measuring and changing position, fearing that without intervention she'd be stuck in there forever, we made our move.

My husband smiled. The doula frowned. I surrendered. Nurses shaved me and counted instruments, then rolled me to the operating room. Suddenly I felt a sharp popping sensation unlike the slow and steady agony of labor. When I told the doctors about it, eyes opened wide and the surgeon ordered the nurse to check the baby's heart rate. Again.

"You're going under," the doctor snapped. I watched the mask cover my nose and mouth.

～ා～

Before I was fully aware, someone handed me a wriggly, sweet smelling bundle. Her fresh skin peeked out at me from beneath pink flannel. She squirmed in my arms and arched her disproportionately large head toward my breast.

I couldn't have planned it better.

Making Babies: Oh, the Glamour!

I HAD MY LAST BABY WHEN I WAS THIRTY. AND WHEN I SAY LAST, I mean that's it. I won't be one of those women taking prenatal vitamins and Boniva at the same time. I don't have the energy.

I waited until the ripe old age of twenty-eight to have my first child, then followed up with a second only twenty-two months later. I had to work quickly because way back then we were afraid to get pregnant after thirty-five. A lot has changed in the last ten years. Pregnancy over forty is now accepted and, if you believe the celebrity photos, easy.

As I inch toward forty, the biological clock still ticks. Instead of, "have-a-baby-have-a-baby," it now says, "just-one-more-just-one-more." I fantasize that I'd do everything right this time. I would coordinate perfect outfits, offer only breast milk and homemade organic baby food, and bathe myself every day. I'd even blow out my hair and put on makeup.

I indulge this dream for about a minute before I remember the

LELA DAVIDSON

sleepless nights, continuous feeding, and emotional extremes. Between post-partum, PMS, and peri-menopause, I can't imagine what older moms—even celebrities—are going through, but I suspect if you knocked on their doors at nine in the morning, they wouldn't be red carpet ready.

Despite the realities of baby rearing, glitz and ease is exactly what we see in those magazines we sneak read at the grocery checkout. People complain that Hollywood glamorizes young pregnancy by holding up Jamie Lynn Spears and Ashlee Simpson as role models, but I'm more offended by the forty-is-the-new-twenty-two celebrities that are selling us regular women a bill of goods.

- Gorgeous Naomi Watts gave birth to a second son at age forty. She claims to have lost all her baby weight breast feeding. I'm sure it had nothing to do with her live-in personal chefs and trainers.

- Over-forty Australian actress Rachel Griffiths plays an American on *Brothers and Sisters*. She's pregnant with her third baby and like our homegrown celebs, she has a penchant for unique names. She already named one son Banjo. Let's hope age has wised her up. If not, she may end up with a cute little Fiddle or Harmonica.

- Desperate Housewife Marcia Cross gave birth to twin daughters at age forty-five. Seriously? At least she'll be able to use her AARP travel discount to take them on their senior trip.

◎ Supermodel Stephanie Seymour had another baby at forty. Paparazzi caught her frolicking in the surf. Is it wrong to hate her? There's not enough Pilates in the world to get me into a bikini post-childbirth—and I started young.

◎ Perhaps the wisest is none other than the daughter of the King himself, Lisa Marie Presley. She welcomed twin girls at age forty. She had the foresight to birth two other children sixteen and nineteen years ago, so now she's got live-in childcare. Now that's planning ahead.

~☙~

I'd love to see these A-listers before their morning triple tall latte. Show me the beautiful people frantically chasing down a toddler, trying to get neon poop out of the carpet, and dripping in spit up. Then I'll be impressed.

My advice? If you're planning to get pregnant over forty, do yourself a favor and cancel your subscription to *People* magazine.

If I Had Tweeted My Labor

I AM A LITTLE ADDICTED TO MY SOCIAL NETWORKS, ESPECIALLY Facebook. I'm not alone. I love these updates so much it almost makes me wish I could have another baby.

Almost.

I like to think I'd exercise restraint if I were having a baby in this social media-saturated world, but who am I kidding? I'd be so much worse than a few Facebook updates. I would Twitter the whole thing.

OMG! Just started timing contractions. Totally on schedule. This is going to be soooo great. Can't wait to start breathing exercises!

I <3 #childbirth!

Contractions R starting to hurt. Husband wants 2 go 2 the hospital but I'm calling the doula. No drugs! #naturalchildbirth

Wow this hurts! Breathing exercises not providing much relief.

Contractions are WAY worse than in pictures.

Threw up on the way to hospital. Husband totally freaking out. #natural childbirth ?

Trying to Tweet in the tub w/o wrecking phone. #pain

Laboring in water = overrated. Tub now freezing but it hurts too bad to get out. WTF? Who thought of this?

Way better now. Drugs will do that. Something with 'cain' in the name took the edge off. LOL Waiting for my #epidural!

Dr. Feelgood just asked if I was in the middle of a contraction! ROTFLMAO! I'll show him a contraction!

Epidurals=NOT overrated!!

9.5? WTF is 9.5? When is this monster going 2 get out of me? Seriously, suck this thing out NOW!"

Totally should have gotten that one final pedicure. #vanity

I give up. They're shaving me now. Getting this kid out one way or another. K, the other way… #cesarean

Does anyone speak anesthesiologist? What part of 'Yes, I can feel that' does he not understand?!?!?!?!?!?!?!

⚬

I know I would have been unceremoniously separated from my phone before the actual moment of birth, but it would have been worth it. I mean, just think of how many new followers I'd get.

Confessions of an Earth Mama Wannabe

I WAS PREGNANT IN SEATTLE, WHERE I SHOPPED AT TRADER JOE'S, grew herbs on my condo lanai, and reused the protective sleeves on my piping hot lattes. I tried to be an Earth Mama, I really did. Before my son was born I was determined to attempt cloth diapers. Yes, *attempt*. Not exactly committed to the cause, but taking credit for the effort.

I might have been stronger in my conviction for green diapering had I not been privy to the memory of my mother hunched over a putrid white bucket, rinsing a thick septic mess of my brother's nappies. However, we'd come a long way since the stinking 70s. In my 1998 urban existence I had access to something my mother never could have imagined or afforded from the secluded farmhouse of my childhood: diaper service. With support I could be a Good Mother, an Earth Mama even.

I could try, anyway.

It might have gone down differently if not for the circumcision.

Like most of my contemporaries, I had my baby boy snipped shortly after his birth. On the West Coast, this—along with not eating the placenta, or at least planting it in the yard under a Very Special Tree—put a serious pall on my potential for environmentally friendly mothering. I would have to pick a lot of blackberries in the park, do hours of yoga, and eat buckets full of granola to make up for this crime.

At the nurses' suggestion—to avoid diaper rash on his extra-Extra-EXTRA sensitive parts—we used disposable diapers for the first week at home. Throwaway Velcro was my friend, as was the space age mock-cotton that held about a gallon of "liquid." Eager to prove my nature-loving worthiness, I circled the two-week mark on the calendar and called the service to schedule my initial delivery. On the big day I received a ten-foot stack of new diapers and a contraption for storing the soiled ones. The next week they would swap out the used for fresh.

I quickly got to work trying out the new diapers. My son humored me, lying calmly through my struggles with the intricate diaper origami. Ten years ago you needed an engineering degree to maneuver a cloth diaper. My son and I blew through four outfits that afternoon, in part because of the gaping diaper-to-skin issues, and partially because my dear progeny refused to pace himself.

Still, I was determined. Right up until it came time to pack for a weekend trip away. I calculated the number of diapers I'd need for the two-day trip and piled them on the bed. Turns out you go through a lot more cloth diapers than disposable because, in contrast to their Earth-ravaging counterparts, reusable diapers hold approximately a quarter teaspoon of pee. I filled an entire suitcase with the mountain of diapers. I sighed, crossed my arms, squinted, huffed. Then I took the diapers out of the suitcase, loaded them back into the sack in which they had arrived, and called the service.

"This just isn't working out."

"Ma'am, don't you at least want to give it until the end of the day?"

"It's been six hours. I get it."

It was not the first time in my brief tenure as Mother that I realized things would not always proceed as planned. But the pacifier incident is another story.

One-fourth of a day. Not bad for an herb-growing, latte-sipping, ozone-destroying Earth Mama Wannabe.

The Legend of My Ten-Pound Baby

DESPITE THE EVER-INCREASING RESPONSIBILITIES, THERE ARE NO promotions in motherhood. You'll never get an annual review followed by a fat bonus and a healthy raise. There's a once-a-year day of gratitude, but the rest of the time we take our props where we can. It is not enough that we (almost) singlehandedly grew an entire human being inside our bodies and then managed to keep the little sucker (literally) alive in the face of deadly car seats and crib bars. We value what we can quantify as credit for a job well done.

I earned a gold star for my daughter's birth weight. Despite a carefully constructed birth plan, an ancient Korean midwife's fetal turning technique, and my doula's soothing-sounds-of-the-snow-owl CD, my second child, a precious flannel bundle, had to be pried out of me under anesthesia—with a big knife. She was born gray with an Apgar score of one, and nearly killed us both.

Why? She was a ten-pound baby, that's why. Ten.

Okay, 9 pounds 14 1/2 ounces. I embellished, but when you have a baby that big you're allowed to round up. An ounce and a half isn't an exaggeration; it's a shot of tequila. (Which may have taken the edge off the cheese-grater-on-nipple sensation of breastfeeding.) I'm just saying, it wasn't a big fib. From Day One, my daughter was a 10-pound baby. For the last decade, all my kick-ass-ness as a mother has been implicit when I casually mention, "That one? Ten pounds."

Okay, just under ten pounds. Who's counting?

I would have perpetuated the legend indefinitely, but on her tenth birthday my daughter asked to look at her baby book. This couldn't go well. Surely she'd notice her book consisted of a few good pages, followed by a few more of random baby items, and then two-dozen blanks. I figured as long as we didn't break out the meticulous record of Big Brother's first year for a side-by-side comparison, she might never know that she was conceived primarily as a playmate for our favorite child.

I shouldn't have worried. All she wanted to see was her birth certificate. My husband and I beamed over her shoulder as she flipped through the handful of pages devoted to her first days. Then the trouble started. There on the first page of the sub-standard baby book was her birth announcement, the one I had created with my own breast milk-stained fingers.

"Do you see what I see?" I asked my husband.

"What?""

"Eight pounds fourteen ounces? What is that?"

"What?"

"She weighed ten pounds! Ten! Well, you know, nine fourteen."

Like all smart husbands faced with an unwinnable situation, he shrugged.

How could I have made such a mistake? As I paged through the official documentation, a ten-pound knot formed in my stomach. The hospital record of birth, her crib identification card, and the doula's notes all confirmed her actual birth weight: 8 pounds 14 1/2 ounces.

She wasn't just under ten pounds at all. She was just under *nine* pounds. Nine. This fact would not reconcile with my myth. I was a five-foot-one She-Ra, a warrior among women, a ten-pound babymaker!

Now what was I? Just over average? Big deal. And it wasn't just about me. My daughter had bought into my heavy white lie, too. The thought of her infant self as bigger than the rest had built up her self-image as a tough girl, maybe even helped her become the best defenseman on her ice hockey team. The facts presented in that stupid baby book shattered all that.

"You mean I wasn't ten pounds?"

My daughter looked like I'd just wiped out the entire balance of her iTunes account.

"I don't care what it says," my husband told her. "You'll always be a ten pounder to me." He glanced in my direction. "And don't worry, Babe. Your secret's safe."

So, the legend will live on, but somehow I don't feel right about keeping that gold star.

Forgive Us Our Sins

Shortly after my husband's employer moved our family to a small Texas town, we decided our eighteen-month old daughter needed saving, as in baptism. We visited several congregations and settled on a quaint Episcopal church. After a respectable period of near-weekly attendance, we asked the rector to christen our youngest. He agreed, but not without a price: Father Bob wanted to talk to us—at our house.

If letting kids overdose on TV was the original sin of parenting, DVDs have pushed us to a new level of depravity. Despite my strict limits on video games, sugary cereal and television, when I needed to buy time for a worthy task—like chatting up the priest—I relied on kid-friendly movies. So on a frosty December evening my husband popped in *Shrek* and joined me in the living room with Father Bob.

"Eggnog?" I offered.

Father Bob hesitated. "I'd better not."

Bob was a forty-something ex-computer guy from Silicon Valley with a lawyer wife and three long-haired sons. I expected him to be cool like the martini-sipping-tai-chi-doing priest who'd baptized our son in Seattle. I also expected small talk. I was wrong on both counts.

"Baptism is permanent," Father Bob began. "It symbolizes our union with Christ."

From the next room the soundtrack roared:

"Look at me! I'm a flyin' donkey!"

Giggles exploded, but Father Bob ignored the interruption. "In baptism your daughter will be washed clean of sin."

My husband said we should wait until after college. Father Bob shifted in his seat. He then spoke of water and oil for what seemed like eternity. "She will be sealed in the mystical Body of Christ."

I emptied my eggnog. "We were hoping for sometime in January?"

"Spring perhaps," said Father Bob.

While he continued to speak of holy things, I counted to ten inside. It's not like we hadn't done this before. We knew the drill: pray-sprinkle-pray-eat-done. Pencil in a date already! After another twenty minutes of reverence I was about to reach for his calendar myself. I heard *Shrek's* blaring guidance:

"Relax, Donkey!"

Nothing fazed Father Bob. He resumed the deep thoughts, but my husband and I had no more energy to mm-hmm and ah-ha. At this rate my daughter would never join the community of the church—or whatever he said. We tried to listen respectfully until an especially ill-timed moment of silence sealed her fate. In Dolby Stereo, our hero, Shrek, proclaimed his noble intention to rescue Donkey:

"I've got to save my ASS!"

Tight, closed-mouth smiles circled the room. Our daughter's mortal soul was clearly in danger and only Father Bob could help.

"Next Sunday?" he asked.

And just like that, the gates of paradise opened, despite our many, many sins. With happy, occupied children, I refilled my eggnog and said goodbye to Father Bob, who had our name on his calendar—in ink.

The Terrible Twos, Give or Take a Few

But Why?

SHE BELLIED UP TO THE BAR IN STARCHED WHITE COTTON.

"Why are private parts private?" my daughter asked.

This is how it began, over cornflakes and before coffee.

"Yeah, Mom," my son joined in. "Why *are* private parts private?" He stared me down.

I pride myself on reasonably articulate responses:

Where do babies come from?

Love.

How does the baby get into the Mommy?

Daddy-seed-Mommy-God.

How? Is there a hole?

Who wants to go to Krispy Krème?

This particular morning my children had me trapped like a barkeeper in an old western—two rugged cowpokes getting to the bottom of things, and little old me pouring milk and making sandwiches. I stalled, waffled, and willed my brain to lasso an answer. I repeated the question, mumbled slowly, and thought aloud.

Why are private parts private?

"Well... they're private... they... they're... um, special... they're private *because* they're special...."

I heard whistling and I swear I saw a tumbleweed roll by outside. Lacking a real answer I fell back on my litany about looking, touching and keeping your private parts private. I reminded them to scream and run.

"Even a piano teacher could be a bad man," my son said.

Ouch.

I am so, so sorry Mr. Wonderful Music Teacher. I'm sure you are a good man, but you sit close to my son on that bench and I am obligated to teach him about scary things because I am a Mother. It's in the job description.

"Yeah, Mom, we know all that," my daughter persisted, "but *why* are private parts private?"

I sighed.

"They have Very Special Purposes."

"Like going to the bathroom?" my son said.

"Exactly."

"And wiping, that's important," my daughter added.

"Very."

Then my boy said it: vagina.

I can almost say vulva with a straight face and I'm glad my children know the proper words for their anatomy, but I believe the V-Word is reserved for girls to say. Girls—and boy doctors.

When my son clarified that he didn't have one, my daughter countered: "Well, if you cut off that long thingy, you would."

Insert the big sigh.

I stood alone on the great divide, matching ham and turkey sandwiches to cracker-cheese-peanut-butter-snack-packs. Part of me was proud my children felt free to ask anything, but another part wanted to crawl into the set of *Leave It To Beaver*, to answer simply with "because", and take my June Cleaver ass to the club to throw back a double martini.

It would have been nice to be preparing these answers all along.

I wished that when I'd left the hospital with my first flannel bundle, they'd handed me a big book of questions my kids would one day ask so I could've gotten a head start. Like those health books they give you. I can't count the number of nights I've searched, bleary-eyed, matching symptoms to illnesses, living for those flow charts. Is the child feverish? No – proceed with home treatment. Yes – call your doctor, NOW!

I wasn't asking for answers, just questions to ponder:

Why does the grass grow up?

Where does the Tooth Fairy live?

Who made God?

Just a little help to navigate the wide-open spaces of parent-hood.

My children's question haunted me for a week until, finally, I gave up. I don't have all the answers, and that's okay. I'm sure they'll learn plenty more out on the prairie. I only hope my children always come home, stare me down until I fess up—best as I'm able, and never stop asking why.

Play Dating

I'M NOT A FAN OF PLAY DATES. I'VE TRAINED MYSELF TO CALL OTHER mothers and schedule time for their children to eat my food and mess up my house, but if it were up to me I'd send my kids into the street to find a friend. As my kids get older, though, I'm faced with a new kind of play date: coed.

It started when my son came home from school excited about a certain girl he'd been partnered with on a field trip. Sitting together and giggling, they became more than friends. "It's a very exciting relationship," my son said. Before I could process this information he added a juicy tidbit. "We're either going to Hawaii or the Bahamas for our honeymoon—so she can wear those coconuts on her nipples."

I was speechless.

"Sorry, breasts," he said. Like that was better.

I pushed the honeymoon thing out of my mind until later that night when my little boy asked for my engagement ring. *Yeah, right—as soon as your dad upgrades me to the two carat.*

Things were moving fast, but I appreciated the upside. The same hormones causing my son to smell like a hamper were now making him like girls enough to want to lose that stink. When he showered, the intoxicating aroma of AXE body wash and spray filled the house. In terms of grooming, we're working on "less is more." But if I wanted information, and the more the better, I had to play it cool.

"What do you call it when you like someone and they like you back?" I asked when I tucked him in that night.

"The other kids call it being a couple," he said. "But I don't like that."

Oh, good.

"Because we're still just getting into each other."

He had a point.

"Can we have a play date?"

I wondered about the protocol. Do I call the mom? Does he call the girl? Can I send them to the playroom like I do with the rest of the neighborhood rugrats or do I have to chaperone?

The next day I called the mother and invited the girl over to play. I even invited the little brother to come along to make it less of a date, only that didn't quite worked out like I planned. Now he and my daughter are engaged too.

"We're getting married," she said, flashing me the Ring Pop she received as a promise.

I'll have to get used to it, this passage from play dates to dating, from dating to rings. And when the big moments come, I hope I'll be able to let go gracefully. I hope, too, that my daughter will hold out for the two carat. On second thought, a candy ring isn't so bad. It's big, it's showy, and when you break up, you can eat it.

Let Them Eat Cake

APPARENTLY MARIE ANTOINETTE NEVER EVEN SAID IT, BUT I WILL. I'm talking birthday parties. Forego the fancy and just let them eat cake.

When my daughter was three, she went to a party at a gymnastics studio—one of those event parties that serve the dual purposes of placating the spoiled rottens for two hours and showing off the family resources.

Hooray.

Forty kids balanced, jumped, and flew through the air. When the time came for opening gifts, the birthday girl sat on a throne—yes, a throne—while her mother ripped open packages and shoved them into the girl's lap. The father digitally captured his princess's indifferent dismissal of dolls, puzzles, and games while the mother screamed out names to be recorded by yet another of the child's staff.

A gift without a card wreaked havoc:

"DORA?" the mother screamed out to the crowd. "WHO GAVE THE DORA?" She huffed and rolled her eyes when no one answered, but the show had to go on.

Birthday parties are out of control. The kid lived another year. Get over it. If you don't stop now, by the time she's fifteen your royal one will need an international audience in Times Square to feel appreciated.

For both of my children's first birthdays we invited hordes of friends, family, and neighbors for BBQs. There were special baby cakes for smashing and kegs next to the helium machine. I made invitations and food from scratch. The first birthday is all about the parents—as it should be. You deserve to show off the fact that you, a mere mortal, have managed to keep an infant alive for an entire twelve months. Go ahead; celebrate like it's 1999!

After Year One, tone it down. Don't worry about the kids. They're not as interested in being popular and impressing their friends as you are. They just want to eat cake.

Mellowing out your own kids' parties is a good start, but it's not enough. Sadly, some people won't comply with my simple request to the excise the excess. That's why there's another side to this plan. In addition to toning down your child's parties, you'll also need to transform him into an unwanted guest to cut down on the number of adorable invites littering his inbox—I mean cubby. It's as easy when you coach your kids to say the right things.

Instead of:

Happy birthday, Johnny. Thank you for having me.

Teach this:

I hope you like your water gun. The kids who made it are about our age. I'm glad we don't live in China.

Instead of:

Thank you, Mrs. Smith, for inviting me to the party.

Try this:

Wow, look at all this wrapping paper—good thing we've got so many landfills.

Or this:

Don't feel bad about throwing out all that food. I don't think kids in Africa even like pizza.

You get the idea. In no time your kid will be blacklisted from every birthday party in town. Double bonus—no gifts to buy and no reciprocal invitations! Think of how good it'll feel to reclaim your Friday nights and Saturday afternoons.

When it's your turn to host you can blindfold the little brats, put something sharp in their hands, and spin them around until they're dizzy. That's what our parents did. Kids don't mind, so long as you feed them cake afterward.

Health Nut

RECENTLY I HAD ONE OF THOSE AFTERNOONS. TOO MUCH homework, multiple sports practices, deadlines, and a child so stricken with allergies that he could neither breathe nor see. I dreaded adding, "make dinner," to my responsibilities, so I did what people do.

"Let's order pizza," I said to my daughter, the one without eyes the size of boiled eggs. She tilted her badly-in-need-of-washing head. You see, because I am such a Good Mommy, because I cook meals almost every night with multiple food groups in pretty colors, and because we rarely eat out, my daughter had no idea what I was talking about.

"You can order a pizza?"

Seriously? What kind of six-year-old freak had I raised who didn't know that pizza comes from a zit-faced teenager who shows up at your house in a run down Hyundai without insurance? I pride myself on being honest with my kids, teaching them about the real world. Clearly, I had failed because in the real world people order pizza.

In my desire to keep my kids from becoming gluttons for junk food, I'd become a glutton for my own kitchen punishment. Worse, I'd sheltered them from an important reality: sometimes we dial up a meal. There's no shame in that. I wondered if my health consciousness—while instilling great habits for the future—was also sucking the life out of their childhood. This wasn't the first time I'd overshot the nutrition target.

When my kids were about four and two we went to a Halloween party where they were offered Kool-Aid.

"What's that?" my son asked.

In her best Texas drawl, my friend consoled, "Y'all don't know what Kool-Aid is?" She gave me the slit eye before turning her charm on my babies. "Let's go get you some."

It wasn't my fault. I'm actually quite moderate considering mossy Pacific Northwest origins. On the West Coast it is not uncommon for children to exist on soymilk, tofurkey, and fresh pressed carrot juice. Sesame nuggets and carob-covered raisins are indulgent snacks for kids up and down Interstate 5. Even the baked corn chips in my pantry would have been shunned by my earthier contemporaries.

Being the healthy mom isn't all sunshine and sprouts. Some-times I'd like to dole out donuts and Hot Pockets, to say yes to shakes and fries. I'm sad when neighbor kids run from my sugar free popsicles and won't eat my ham and green bean enhanced macaroni and cheese.

My husband found me cooking dinner the other day.

"Oh you really hate those kids, don't you?"

"What do you mean?" I asked as I breaded a tilapia fillet.

"Fish and Brussels sprouts?"

I wanted to silence him with a broccoli spear, but my fingers were crusted with breading. "Watch it," I warned. "I still have time to cook brown rice."

He jokes, but my kids love veggies, especially the cruciferous one. Or maybe they've learned that they can't beat me, so they may as well join me. I have trained them well. My children keep Halloween candy for months; we throw out ice cream because we forget to eat it; they choose water over juice boxes, love cauliflower, and they have never, to my knowledge, consumed a fruit roll up.

Freaks?

Maybe.

Perfect little eaters?

I'd like to think so.

However, my belief that we're creating lifelong habits here in my healthy kitchen was dashed when I caught one of the children eating a booger the other day. Apparently my snacks are so bad they've turned to the salty satisfaction of nasal discharge. At least boogers are all natural.

On second thought, maybe pizza and PopTarts aren't so bad after all.

Sex, Drugs, and Jesus

I RECENTLY TOLD MY SON HOW THE BABY GETS INTO THE MOMMY. It may have been early, but I figure at nine he's halfway to college and I'm pretty sure he'll find out there. Plus he'd been asking, a lot.

I made a date with him to throw down the facts. Then I got cold feet and wondered if his dad shouldn't be the one to do the honors. But my husband isn't good with gory details. Besides, he was out of the country and the cell tower gods wouldn't cooperate. To prevent myself from chickening out, on the drive to the coffee shop I told my son I was finally going to tell him about where babies come from. When he started asking questions I whipped out the old answer-with-a-question technique.

"Well, how do you think the baby gets in there?"

"I know about the eggs and seeds, but how do the seeds get in there?"

"I think you know enough."

He shook his head.

Once we'd settled into Starbucks and found a seat outside, I tried to squirm out of it again. I stalled, reminding him that this wasn't something he needed to talk about with his friends.

"Come on, Mom. Tell me."

I took a deep breath, surprised at how uncomfortable I had become. "Okay so you know that the seed fertilizes the egg right?"

"Yeah, just like animals."

"Yes, exactly like animals."

"Then what?"

I swallowed. "That's basically it."

"But how does the seed get into the Mommy?"

It suddenly became difficult to breathe.

"Well," I said, "the Daddy puts the seed into the Mommy."

"How?"

Oh my God, with the questions! Breathe – Relax – Breathe.....

"Well, you know how private parts are special right?"

"Yeah."

"You know how a baby comes out?"

"From here," he said, putting his hand on his crotch.

"From a girl."

"Yeah, I know that." Duh.

"So private parts are for?" Maybe if I could make him say it, I wouldn't have to.

"Going to the bathroom and babies?"

"Right. So if a girl's private parts are for going to the bathroom and babies, what do you think a boy's private parts are for?"

"Peeing?"

"And?"

"Babies?"

"Yes."

"I don't get it."

And here I thought this kid was supposed to be smart. I drew a deep breath and took the plunge.

"The seed comes from your penis."

"O-kaaaaaay," he said. "But I still don't know how it gets into the Mommy."

I took a very deep breath and held onto my chair. "The-daddy-puts-his-penis-into-the-mommy's-vagina."

"GROSS!"

"I know! It's totally gross!"

"Mom, that's disgusting!"

"You're right. It is."

He was starting to grin. "But when you grow up and get married and want to have a baby it won't seem so gross. I promise."

He seemed to accept this. "So that's it?"

"That's all. That's sex."

When we called his Dad to tell him what we'd learned, my son said, "I'm probably too young to know this, but Mom just told me how the baby gets into the Woman."

Now it's Woman? What happened to Mommy?

He whispered into the phone, "Did you really have to put your you-know-what into Mommy's you-know-what?"

The agony.

"Ask if he has anything to add," I said.

After a few minutes my son handed me the phone.

"He's all grown up," my husband said. "I think his voice is changing."

We hung up and I explained how kids are going to tell him all kinds of crazy things, but I'll always tell him the truth. I reminded him that he could always ask me anything.

"There's a lot of confusion out there," I said. "Some people will try to trick you, and other kids are just dumb. You need to come to me for all the important information."

And in one evening, we went from "Come on, Mom, tell me" to "Yeah, yeah, Mom—sex drugs, and Jesus—I get it."

Cut Costs This Year, Starting with the Tooth Fairy

IF YOU'RE STINGING FROM THE PAIN OF THE ECONOMIC DOWNTURN or suffering nasty paper cuts from your post-holiday credit card statements, consider cutting back on child-related costs this year. Examine your budget carefully, and wisely wield your scalpel. If you vow to say no to peer pressure of the imaginary kind this year, you may find the Tooth Fairy budget is ripe for cutting.

When my daughter lost her first tooth, she was handsomely rewarded by the Tooth Fairy with a crisp dollar bill (which I swiped from my son's piggy bank, but that's another story). The next morning she pranced down the stairs, proud of her newfound riches. A whole dollar! She couldn't have been happier.

A couple of days later, her mouth got in the way of two toddlers engaged in a friendly backyard brawl. She ran bleeding and triumphant across the lawn, showing off the fresh gape at the bottom of her Kindergarten smile.

That evening as I put her to bed, she placed the tooth carefully under her pillow.

"Mom?" Her little face shone, full of hope.

"Yes, Sweetie?" I said, pulling up the sheet and folding it under her chin.

Her eyes grew large. "Some people get more than a dollar."

Knowing where this was going, I tried not to react. "Really? What do they get?"

She hesitated before answering. "Well… some people get toys." She turned shy—or was it calculating—before adding, "Ella got twenty dollars."

Twenty bucks? For a tooth? No wonder the economy is a mess.

I told my daughter that I didn't know Ella's arrangement, nor anything about the official Tooth Fairy payment schedule, but that her brother had always received one dollar from the irrepressible imp, and that she ought to expect the same.

Not to deprive the Tooth Fairy of her mission in life, but consider for a moment where this kind of inflation leads. If you let the Tooth Fairy drop twenty dollars a pop, then what about the Easter Bunny? He won't be upstaged by some flighty chick who doesn't even merit her own holiday. Before you know it, the gold bunny will be made of actual gold.

I don't mind if other parents choose to buy every impulse snack and toy in the checkout. I humor the birthday parties with magicians, princesses, and ponies, where children garner more gifts than my first twelve Christmases combined. I accept that Valentine's Day and Easter have been elevated to gift holiday status. But don't mess with the Tooth Fairy. When I was a kid, the going rate was a quarter. Just a gesture really. The real thrill of the event was the thing coming out, especially so if there were bloodshed.

Twenty dollars? Seriously?

Poor Santa is already on the hook for plenty. Let this kind of spending go unchecked and mark my words, next year you'll be pulling out a home equity loan for the Valentine's treats. If you can get credit, that is.

Bottom line: It's a tooth, not an accomplishment. Stick to one dollar and if your kid complains, blame it on the Fairy.

The Case of the Easter Bunny

I ADMIT IT: I CAN'T WAIT UNTIL THE EASTER BUNNY STOPS HOP-
ping by our house. It's not that I don't like holidays; I just can't
take the pressure of being the responsible adult. The trouble
with children is that you can't put much over on them, especially
when they seem to be on the elementary school track for pre-
pre-law.

One Easter Eve a few years ago, I lay in bed trying to fall asleep
amid some low level tension because something just wasn't
quite right. Suddenly I bolted up, frightening my husband out
of a sound snore.

"I forgot to do the Easter baskets!"

I got up, turned on lights, rummaged through the guest room
closet for baskets and candy, and set about making the sweetest
little tokens of love from the Easter Bunny. I put them in the
kids' doorways and went back to bed, where the father of my
children was sleeping just as peacefully as before my crisis.

In the morning the kids came to our room to show us their loot. My six-year-old daughter looked up at me with genuine curiosity. "I wonder why the Easter Bunny gave us the same baskets as last year?"

Note: The Easter Bunny is a touch stingy. She doesn't really see the point in buying new baskets year after year, and this was the year she decided to test her theory that the kids wouldn't really notice anyway.

"Mom?" my daughter asked, "Are you the Easter Bunny?"

Leave it to the little one.

I shook my head and offered up a little snort. "Do I look like I've been out all morning hopping around delivering Easter baskets?"

She eyed me, weighing whether or not to push it. She possessed a sparkly bag of sugar, after all. However, the little lawyer-in-training just couldn't let it go. "It's just that you said the Easter Bunny was a girl and the Easter Bunny knows what kind of books we like and—"

Maybe Mommy needed a basket full of Midol because I snapped. "I'm not the Easter Bunny. Okay?"

Everybody backed off the bunny. When they asked later why the Easter Bunny didn't give them very much candy this year, I told them maybe she knew they'd be getting a lot of candy at the Easter egg hunt that afternoon.

"Not that I would know," I added.

That was my fatal mistake. If this were a courtroom drama, there would be a close up on me as a bead of sweat made its way down my nose.

"Are you sure you're not the Easter Bunny?" my son asked. His eyes narrowed. "Because usually when people say 'not that I would know,' it means that they know."

"And usually when a kid asks too many questions about a basket of goodies, it means they go to bed early and a monster comes in the night and eats all their candy."

Case closed.

Trotting Out My Turkey

IN THE THIRD GRADE, MY SON'S CLASS PUT ON A THANKSGIVING program in which he starred as both a turkey and a rapper, and read an essay he wrote entitled, "Why I'm Thankful for My Education." I value overachievement, so it was comforting to see my son following my example of excellence. As it turned out, he wasn't the only one expected to perform.

Two weeks before the show, I received a note from the music teacher informing me that my child had been chosen to be a turkey. (Chosen! Nothing better than having my child singled out for special assignments!) Consequently I needed to cover a white t-shirt completely with feathers. Completely: all caps, bold. Use a hot glue gun, it said. If I was not able to make the costume, I was told in a condescending tone, I should call the music teacher immediately.

Ordinarily I'm not interested in proving my worth or competing with other women via my child. (Shoes and bags are more fun.) However, I also can't seem to back away from a challenge. In my fervor for accomplishment, I interpreted this note as a dare.

If I sound—I don't know… possessed?—I blame my mother, who probably couldn't tell you what the letters in PTA stand for. Not that she wasn't supportive in her way. She came to all my plays and concerts and even honored my wish that she not wear sequins, most of the time. The woman just wasn't PTA material. I think there's a gene for it. So in my extended adolescent rebellion to be not-like-my-mother, I skipped off like a Good Mommy to the local big box craft store.

To my surprise, an entire aisle of the store was devoted to feathers. Turns out they are not cheap, especially turkey-appropriate colors like brown, white, and black. I attributed the lower price point of the bolder colors to less demand. (The cul-de-sac burlesque scene wasn't exactly "happening.") I compromised, buying one packet of suitable feathers and a value pack for filler. How badly could a fuchsia and chartreuse turkey stand out from the crowd anyway?

I moved on to the t-shirt aisle and picked up a child's small in "natural." I figured the color would mask any ill effects of my feather scrimping. If I happened to run out of feathers mid-wing, my son would have a turkey-ish color showing through. I congratulated myself on this improvement over the suggested white.

That night I waited impatiently for the glue to melt in the barrel of my trusty, but ancient, glue gun. Then I got to sticking. Sure, I attached the first few feathers to my own shirt and yes, I burned off two fingerprints, but overall, for a virgin turkey costume designer, I rocked it. After thirty minutes, I called it good, even if there were a few spots of natural showing through.

Able? I'll show them able!

The feedback I got the next day after the Thanksgiving Extravaganza dress rehearsal, suggested otherwise.

"You forgot the sleeves," a neighbor girl noticed. As if turkey legs have feathers.

"Pink feathers are for princesses," came the next critique.

"There's boogers on it," said a kid who clearly did not understand the physics of dried hot glue.

And those were just the kids. The real assessment of my merit as a mother was yet to come. Those super PTA moms would surely notice that I in fact, did not rock the turkey costume. But my son, ever the encourager, told me not to worry. He pointed out that one kid had worn a plain t-shirt. Plain! That proved I'd done a better job than at least one mom.

On show day, as I took my seat in the cafeteria, tens of turkeys graced the bleacher stage. One actually looked like a very large turkey. A few evoked Vegas acts. The rest looked like mine—scrappy kids with feathers glued to their shirts. My son was not the most attractive faux fowl, but—objectively—his "Turkey Boogie" blew the others kids out of the barnyard. And, not to brag or exaggerate, but his essay demonstrated his ability to lead the free world one day.

Satisfied, relieved, redeemed—I enjoyed the program, distracted only for a moment by my pity for all those other moms, the competitive ones whose kids had no t-shirt showing through.

Pink President

MY SIX-YEAR-OLD AND I WERE WATCHING AMERICA'S NEXT TOP Model the other day—because there's really nothing wrong with that. A girl's got to have role models, after all. While I was feeling a teeny bit guilty about exposing my baby to a world of snorting and gagging, she sprung it on me:

"Can I be a model?"

"Sure you can," I said. "You can be anything." I went into Lame Mom damage control mode, grasping for examples to counter the effects of the models, not to mention Paris Hilton and Lindsay Lohan. Sure, I could have pointed to political figures, but let's be realistic. We were watching Bravo, not CSPAN, and that wasn't exactly an anomaly.

Loudly, aggressively, the ideal heroine came to mind. In all her tatted rebel rock star glory, the answer was Pink. She was perfect! Despite her profanity, I wanted to pipe Pink's message into my daughter's brain while she slept. Independence, unfettered expression, and a complete irreverence for authority. Oh wait, that last one could be troublesome. But yes, that's what I wanted for my girl. Granted it could pose some problems from say, fourteen to twenty-two, but prudence be damned! Ultimately I'd like to raise a girl who knows how to use her voice and get what she wants.

At the same time, the manicured, suburban part of me wanted to shield my baby from—or at least provide unnecessary explanations for—Pink's ink and Kool-Aid colored hair. But these are part of what makes her unique and not a copy of something she saw in a magazine. Upsetting too was all that partying. What if my daughter took Pink's example literally, embracing a life of rock and roll, someday "settling down" with a rock star? I pondered a fantasy future as Steven Tyler's mother-in-law.

I was torn between encouraging my girl to be herself and guiding her along the "right" path.

All I know is that when I crank Pink and hurl out the obscenities along with her, I don't care what anybody thinks. That's what I want for my daughter—sans the sailor mouth, of course. I wanted her to have an answer when someone whispered behind her back: Who does she think she is?

But I couldn't say all that. Not to a first grader. So I instead I put on some lipstick, and blah-blah-blahed about women and society and important jobs and maybe, just maybe, a woman President very soon.

My daughter's eyes popped.

"I'll be President," she said, leaving me feeling redeemed.

"And if nobody votes for me—" she added brightly. "—I'll be a model."

With that I gave up trying to instill any moral authority and went back to watching Top Model. If the girl decides to walk the runway, at least I can take partial credit.

Thanks for the Whore Barbie

DEAR MOM,

Thank you for sending the Whore Barbie. It really is the perfect gift for an eight-year-old. How clever of you to find a loophole to my rule against Bratz dolls. Your granddaughter has been having a great time playing "Sure you're not a cop?" and "Run, there's my pimp."

Oh, I know, Whore Barbie is a model. And I know models often walk around in black lace micro-mini-skirts, fishnet hose, and thigh-high boots with their hips jutting out and their hands on their asses. But still. Let's call a ho a ho. Sure, the platinum blonde hair evokes Julia Roberts in Pretty Woman, but endearing as the movie was, the hooker-with-the-heart-of-gold plot is tough to explain to a third grader.

Maybe you didn't notice the half-closed eyes, but you couldn't have missed the purple and gold eye shadow and the frosty pink lipstick. The doll's a walking blowjob. And you can't tell me that leopard print purse isn't holding the iPhone she uses to process PayPal payments from the tech-savvy johns.

It's not just me. Whore Barbie's not even allowed to play with her wholesomely anorexic counterparts. It states clearly on the back of the box:

Not for use with other Barbie dolls.

Even Mattel knows she's a whore.

Anyway, thanks again. We're off to play "Find my crack."

The Lousiest Blessing

My stomach dropped when I saw the first sesame seed scurry into my daughter's fluffy mop of hair. I didn't yet know that the translucent bug foretold a full infestation. That's what lice do.

She had been itching since the first week of school. What I had passed off as dandruff were actually the tiny nits that, untreated, grow into one of the worst pests known to parent-kind.

"Stop scratching," I begged. "People will think you have lice."

Denial is powerful. At first I thought it was irritation from the headbands she'd started wearing. We tossed those out, but she still scratched. I worked prescription eczema cream into her scalp, assuming the skin condition had migrated from her body to her head. No relief. We tried over-the-counter scalp itch medicine. No help.

After a few weeks, I consulted the internet and what I found wasn't pretty. After a few cleansing breaths I asked my daughter to come close to the window so I could have a look. That's when I saw the first louse disappear into her hair.

I called a nurse and learned there was so much to do. I drove immediately to the store for lice-killing shampoo, fine-toothed nit combs, and tea tree oil. I began what would be a ten-day assault on every live and gestating louse in the house. All soft surfaces received lethal doses of scalding water, bleach, and toxic sprays. There were endless loads of laundry, quarantines of stuffed animals, and nightly nit-picking. I combed my daughter's hair into tiny sections under bright lights for hours every evening. When I called my husband, who was working a thousand miles away in Mexico, I made him itch.

It was hell for days.

It was exactly what I needed.

Several months earlier, when my husband started working out of the country, I had quit my job. In limbo and not sure about which direction to take, I'd been feeling stuck and sorry for myself. The worst part was the inactivity. I watched too much TV, yelled at the kids, and didn't want to talk to my friends. I'd gotten into the rut of having no purpose.

Suddenly those lice gave me something important to do. They got my mind off of me and filled my hours with the meaning of simple tasks. I had to destroy every last louse, had to get them out of my daughter's hair, out of our house, and out of her school. I didn't have the luxury of wasting away in worry about what I was supposed to do with my life. I had work to do. And that was a blessing that proved to be the push I needed to climb out of my funk.

People say God works in mysterious ways. I say sometimes God blesses us in ways that are just plain lousy.

Suburban Bliss

We Are Not The Joneses

WHEN THE KIDS WERE THREE AND FIVE, WE MOVED TO A GREEN
corner of Arkansas that is home to Walmart headquarters,
crazed college football fans, and serious suburban bliss.
Summer in our adopted idyllic corner of the world is filled with
SPF 55, backyard barbeque, and Jonesin' to be the Joneses.
Decks are primed and stained, cars washed and waxed, yards
tended like favorite children. We share banana breads and
casseroles, watch each other's children, and mill around one
another's driveways discussing grass.

Like our 1950's predecessors, we yearn for a pristine, Kelly
green Lego lawn. We admire, compare, and criticize the patches
of green that grace our cul-de-sac. We are astounded at the thick
carpet of grass next door and suspect its owner to be a midnight
fertilizer. We strategize ways to even out the bumps, wonder at
the weeds that seem to defy the laws of poison, and share truck-
loads of sand to create level surfaces that last through one
thunderstorm. Peer pressure in this block of green blocks
should be a strong motivator, but the Davidsons are not the

Joneses. Our lawn is not the envy of the lane; in fact, I am actually grateful that it is not the worst.

The humble square of earth in front of my house is lumpy, won't green up, and the edges never come out straight. It is rarely even with the adjacent yards and the unblown clippings accumulate at the edges, combining with the water from the automatic sprinkler to create a green sludge that is unwelcome in a tidy Mid-American subdivision. But the hard-bodied English major who mows it is more interested in his LSAT score than the proper disposition of my excess Bermuda.

Therein lies the problem. A boy—not my husband—cuts our grass. And a boy can never love a lawn as a man ought to. However, the man I married would rather opt out of the Jones chasing altogether. He proudly proclaims to Mr. Jones, "I'll make you look good."

Call it laziness, but he prefers well-adjusted. John simply has better things to do on Saturday afternoon than pamper the lawn and mother the mulch. Do I want to see him shirtless like the twenty-something lawn ornament? Maybe not. Then again, perhaps a little round-the-house with a mower would transform his upper body into something worth leering at.

But I've gone off topic.

The backyard is even worse than the front. John built a huge deck, but the stain he used turned out less than good. He likes to pretend it looks okay.

"What did you put on it?" Mr. Jones asked.

My husband mumbled something unintelligible, even to another of his own kind. When Mr. Jones begged his pardon, my Cro-Magnon only grunted.

"No, really, I want to know," Jones persisted, "So I don't put it on mine."

By the next year, the varnish had flaked and the wood had begun to pucker and warp.

"What are you going to do about it?" asked Mr. Jones. I couldn't tell if he was concerned, sanctimonious, or simply disgusted.

"I'm not going to do anything."

"You can't leave it like this." Yes, that was definitely disgust.

"Sure I can." John grinned. "When I'm ready to sell, I'll slap on a fresh coat."

I told you we were not the Joneses.

This year, at the beginning of deck maintenance season, Mr. Jones mentioned his weekend staining plans.

"Again?" John asked. He still didn't get that, like our anniversary, deck maintenance is an annual event. "Tell you what," he said, "I'll pay you not to stain your deck."

Mr. Jones took a deep, cleansing breath and replied, "Why don't you take that money and hire someone to stain yours for you?"

That's not going to happen. We need the money for the lawn guy. And for the cute little tops I wear while he's doing his sub-standard yard work. And possibly for marriage counseling if the lawn boy ever takes me up on my offer for fresh-squeezed lemonade.

Puppy Love

I'M NO DOG PERSON. I NEVER WANTED THE RESPONSIBILITY OF A puppy, certainly not a male dog. So you can imagine my surprise when I brought home a male puppy.

It all started with an Italian Greyhound I met while waiting in line for my latte at Barnes & Noble. This dog was my soul mate, but the owner would not take a child in trade, so the search was on.

After being denied by a rescue shelter because my children were too young for this supposedly fragile breed, I was nearly talked into a Chihuahua by a smooth pet store operator. Then I spied the ad for an IG puppy—and at only a hundred bucks, a mere pittance of his worth. The kids and I made the forty-five minute trek deep into the country in search of Dog. On the drive out there I reminded them we might not take him home.

"Not if he's not nice," I said. "Or if he smells." You know, like a dog.

The moment we saw him, I had no trouble handing over the five crisp twenties. My precious skinny puppy, my miniature racing-dog peered into me with deep, blue eyes and I took in his gorgeous dogginess. We dubbed him Simon and rushed straight to the pet super store. Everything was cute and fresh, and smelled nice, like school clothes in September.

Nothing is that easy. A week later I lived with a reeking dog bed, hair everywhere, and yellow designs in my carpet. He was worth it, though. We babied our new family member, but I set boundaries. No pet nannies, organic dog food, or doggy cashmere sweaters. No Juicy Couture track suits for this pup. And no dog was licking my face. Never-ever-ever. I would feed him, alter him, and immunize him, but no licking.

There was competition, too. About ten minutes after I brought Simon home, two of my neighbors appeared with puppies. The cul-de-sac became a dog park. Now I've got to keep up with the Dog Joneses.

"My dog never pees inside."

"My dog's poops are small."

"My dog doesn't chew the carpet— did I tell you about my new carpet?"

They can brag all they want, but I know my dog is best because he loves me the most. I know this because when I let him, he snuggles in my lap, arches his visible spine, and places his long snout on my chest.

A supposed watchdog, he barks for only one reason—when he wants me to come to the back door to play psych. It goes like this: "Bark-bark, please let me in, oh please won't you let me in, open the door pleeeeeze." And then when I open the door he prances back on the deck and I swear he smiles. Psych!

He smells bad, has no manners, and he's expensive. I just spent nearly twice his asking price to ensure he doesn't bless anyone else with a puppy. My dog is a complete pain. But it doesn't matter because he's part of our family now. I'm committed. And that reminds me of all the people in my life I am bound to love, too, despite their occasionally annoying habits. Face licking is still out, but my dog has found a way to express affection. He looks at me with those puppy dog eyes and gently places one paw on my cheek, where I let it stay for half a breath before I brush it away.

Surely that doesn't make me a dog person.

Garden Spiders Beware

My BACKYARD LOOKS SHABBIER THAN USUAL. I BLAME SPIDERS, one in particular. He had a big yellow abdomen with black stripes. He was, literally, a garden-variety spider. I'm not proud to admit that I made my kids throw rocks at the web while I watched from the safety of the kitchen.

As most phobias do, my fear of spiders began in childhood. When I was a kid we kept chickens behind the garage and it was my job to collect the eggs. One morning I found a huge, dewy web between my breakfast and me. I marched back to the house and cried to my parents. They armed me with a plastic bowling pin and told me—not in so many words—to face my fears.

I spent the next twenty-five years letting others kill the spiders in my path. After the move to Texas, I had let other people kill the scorpions, too, until one day, on my way out the front door, I met a spider the size of a Volkswagon. It was the blackest, hairiest thing I'd ever seen—a tarantula. I froze. When I backed into the doorway, Spidey took it as an invitation to crawl toward me on the fastest eight legs I'd ever seen. My heart could have jumped out of my chest and back into the house before I did.

Inside, I peeked out the window. No big deal, I told myself. I'd just stay put until it left. One problem: I had a friend coming. She'd have kids with her. I couldn't leave them defenseless against The Beast. Besides, I'd been a mother for three whole years. I was supposed to be tough. I couldn't give in to a spider. I had to kill it.

I filled an empty formula tin with water, opened the door, inched toward the spider, and doused it. Bad idea. I missed the spider completely, but startled it into racing toward me again. I hopped back inside and slammed the door, then slid down the door until I was sitting on the floor. I pulled my hair searching for a solution. You can do this thing, I told myself.

I got a broom, figuring I'd trick the spider by approaching from the other direction. Creeping through the garage and around the house, I wondered why broom handles weren't longer. Closer and closer, I gained confidence. Yes, this was going to work. Closer, just a little closer…

Thwack! Thwack, thwack again. Smush, crush. "Die, you little freak!"

The spider didn't move. That's one good thing about spiders. They wither up and die, not like some pests that play dead, only to skuttle away before you return with a tissue. For good measure, I swept the incapacitated monster into the flowerbed and covered it with dirt. Then I filled the formula tin again and flooded the spot, making a little puddle in the red clay. Bludgeoned, buried, and drowned. Dead for certain.

I dug it up later to show my husband. "It was a lot bigger before I killed it," I told him. He sort of believed me.

You'd think after going medieval on a tarantula so many years ago I'd be over my fear of spiders. I'm not. So when you see my back yard looking neglected, you can blame that yellow and black striped garden-variety fiend. What's my excuse for the front beds? That's where we found the black widow.

Top 10 Things That Could Go Wrong While Baking – A Cautionary Tale

I MAKE COMMENTS IN MY COOKBOOKS WHEN I TRY RECIPES—
things like "Excellent," "Needs more salt," and "Kids loved it."
What I wrote after a recent traumatic cake baking experience is
not suitable for publication. If my cookbooks survive me, it will
be a testament to my descendants of their grandmother's battle
with baked goods, and her potty mouth.

I don't know why I torture myself with baking from scratch. I
ought to stick with recipes printed on the back of a box with a
red spoon in the corner. If you dislike baking—as I do—the
baking knows it, and it messes with you.

Still, me with my optimism, and the deceptively simply recipe
with its butter and eggs…

It was a pound cake. What could possibly go wrong?

For the record:

1. You could be out of flour. Turns out, this is a baking deal breaker. Who knew?

2. You could decide to get some bang for your bake by doubling the recipe. However, now that you have flour, all those ingredients don't neatly fit into your fancy mixer— the one that still matches your kitchen even though you haven't it used since the last time you were delusional enough to bake something, which was a couple of Christmases ago.

3. You could neglect to ask—before getting started—what exactly is a tube pan?

4. You could assume said tube pan is pretty similar to a loaf pan because the name of the recipe has "pound cake" in it, and you've seen pound cakes—plenty of them. They are rectangular, like a loaf pan.

5. You could skim over the part of the recipe that says sift and whip egg whites until they're stiff—whatever that means— and therefore underestimate the time effort, and skill involved in what you thought was going to be your basic dump-stir-pour operation.

6. You could decide that instead of the handy mixer to whip the egg whites, you'll do it by hand, which could result in a nasty cramp in your right bicep.

7. You could ignore the visual evidence that the cake batter does not fit into the aforementioned loaf pan. In fact, you could fill it all the way up so that it's almost spilling out before it even goes into the oven. Then you could be so grateful that the whole drama is in the oven that you don't even mind cleaning up the unholy mess in your kitchen. You might even smile as you're wiping down the last puff of flour.

8. You could smell something familiar: smoke.

9. You could then spend thirty minutes cleaning the scorched batter overflow from the bottom of the oven and transferring partially cooked cake-like material into other pans of various shapes and sizes—none of which are tube pans.

10. You could serve the cake, which despite your monumental incompetence is actually delicious, resulting in rave reviews and requests that you "make this more often."

By the way, in case you're wondering, a tube pan is the same as a Bundt pan and it has a far greater capacity than your average loaf pan. Again, who knew?

Car Trouble

On a hot summer day, while unloading an obscene amount of groceries, I noticed a thick, pink substance on the garage floor. Lemonade? Maybe, but it appeared to be coming from inside the car. After I got my dairy and frozen goods out of the heat, I dipped my finger into the pink mess. It didn't smell like anything and looked about as worrisome as IHOP syrup, which threatens only my thighs.

About an hour later I had to run an urgent errand. If I didn't get that double tall iced latte, someone was getting tied to a tree. Because my husband was out of town, I had another car to drive, one which did not have pink goo oozing out of it. However, I chose to drive the leaky car. It started and drove fine, at first. Soon the thermometer light came on. I tensed when it started to blink, even though I had no idea what that meant.

If I designed cars, there would be a light that said, "Pull Over." And if you didn't immediately comply, another light would come on that said, "NOW!" If you still didn't get the hint, the car would turn itself off. But my car doesn't have this handy imaginary feature. Still, despite the warning light, my trip was uneventful. I finished my urgent errand and drove home.

The next afternoon, after loading the car with five children, four snorkels, two masks, a box of crackers, forty-five fruit snacks, a gross of beach towels, and enough juice to flood a small country, it wouldn't start. I tried again while the children whined, hot and cranky. Clearly this was another urgent situation so I did what I had to do. I switched cars and went to the pool.

Then I had to make the call. "Do you want to hear the bad news?" I asked my husband. I told him about the harmless smelling gunk, the flashing red thermometer, and the non-starting car. Luckily I married a man who remains calm in the face of mechanical trouble.

"Was the car leaking while you were driving?"

"No," I said. "It was in the garage."

"And the light, when was that flashing?"

Here's where things started to turn against me. "Oh, well.... see.... I needed to go to the –"

"You drove the car?"

He is not so calm in the face of four-digit repair bills. I couldn't feed his panic, but had to reassure him that there was nothing to worry about, just a task to accomplish. "What I need to know is whether I should have the car towed to the dealership or if you think we can put in some more of that pink stuff and drive it over."

My husband sighed from another state and I heard the hang of his head. "I hope you didn't seize the engine."

"No." I brushed it off. "I think it's something else—something easy to fix."

Neither my husband nor the mechanic agreed that it was something easy to fix, but it didn't matter. I may not be good with machines, but things always work out for me. For instance, my new car is very shiny.

Rise of My Machines

WE ARE DEPENDENT ON MACHINES: HAIR DRYER, COFFEE POT, television, thermostat, washer, dryer, Toyota, microwave. Too many to list. And sometimes—like after my family watches *The Matrix* for the 412th time—I wonder if we're not getting a little too used to the electrical and mechanical conveniences, if we're not getting too soft.

Foe example, yesterday the dishwasher wouldn't start and my phone froze. That was just the beginning.

After working for two hours, my computer angrily displayed the message that I had better switch over to real power before my battery died. Afraid to lose any portion of the Important Masterpiece I had been writing, I immediately checked everything—the plug that goes into the computer, the black box it feeds into, and the wall socket. All plugged in. My machine made good on its threat and died. I switched outlets. Nothing. Over and over I powered up and the computer shut down, back into hibernation—trying, I assume, to save what little juice was left in its battery. Finally, it made a high pitched wheezing sound and gave up humoring me completely.

I'm dead already!

The black screen stared at me. The blinky-blinky orange light on the power button disappeared. What I had neglected to inspect before—the cord—I now found broken, possibly mistaken for a rawhide by the dog I feed and bathe and medicate.

When I whined to my husband that I was on my way to Best Buy for a new power cord, he told me we had a universal cord in the desk drawer. When I hear the word, "universal," I think of something easy, something equipped with its own internal superior knowledge that allowed it to operate without my help, something even a techno-loser writer could figure out.

Right.

The universal cord had several tips to choose from and several pieces that all seemed to fit together. I eventually figured out the correct order to connect the pieces, but even fully assembled, the master of all power sources wouldn't turn my computer on. I checked the ports again. All were in order so I gave up on the omnipotent power cord and took everything to Best Buy where two guys younger than my Compaq told me I needed a new cord. Perhaps I would like the $149 model. (Not that they're on commission or anything.)

In desperation I visited the Geek Squad desk where I was outrageously lucky to get a wildly talented geek. She listened to my story and offered a few tricks. While she spoke, and without breaking eye contact, she gently turned my computer over, effortlessly located the release, moved the battery slightly, and closed the compartment. Elegantly and without any overt display of ego, she sent me on my way to try the universal cord once more.

At home, the tones of the power-up sequence melted my shoulder tension and let me know that I would live to log in another day. All it had taken was a loving touch.

The machines aren't so different from us after all. I guess that's why we're so dependent on them.

Three Steps to Good Housekeeping

My name is Lela and I have a housekeeper. Don't judge me. I've done enough of that myself. I've also tried to handle the housework myself—even enlisted the kids in a weekly ritual to rid our home of the odor of dog and used Kleenex. The routine consisted of making a list of chores, cranking up the Jonas Brothers, and setting a timer for an hour. It was ugly, but in the end the house was clean—not white glove clean, but good enough.

I would follow up throughout the week nagging the children to pick up their things until I ran out of saliva. This system worked for a while, but the kids complained and I got tired of yelling. We slacked off. When I once again feared picking up a staph infection from my own bathroom, I knew I needed help.

Step 1: Admit that you are powerless over your poor housekeeping.

The grime coating my best wedding gift vase was so thick I'd forgotten its original color; dust bunnies had morphed into a pack of vicious jackrabbits under my sofas; and there were leftovers in the fridge dating back to the Bush Administration. It's like a disease, this inability to scrub grout and polish porcelain. Clearly, I was not in control. So why feel so guilty about outsourcing? I'm only trying to set a good example. I wouldn't want my children to think a woman is supposed to do everything. That would be wrong.

Step 2: Realize that the solution lies in a higher power (i.e. a housekeeper).

I called the woman who used to clean our house back when I had one big paycheck instead of the handful of small ones I now receive. She was available. And she's great—with baseboards, stainless, and my fingerprint-laden glass-topped desk. I justified the luxury by telling myself that now the kids and I will have time to work on the deep detail cleaning and organizing. We'll thwart the landfill-o-crap that threatens to overtake their bedrooms. Mmm-hmmm. That's exactly what we'll do with the time. We won't sit around eating Sour Patch Kids and Raisinettes and watching American Idol. No way.

Step 3: Commence with the cleaning.

Naturally, I had to clean up the house before the housekeeper's first visit. I won't be judged for hair-clogged drains and fuzzy ceiling fans. More important, I don't want her thinking we're trouble like those slobs across the street. I can't afford a rate hike, and I do detest those pesky negotiations.

Her first day back I withheld a giggle as she lemon-polished her way around the room. I let out a hearty "YES" when I saw the neat pile of rags next to the washer after she'd gone. I floated through the house on a lavender and Pledge-scented cloud. Goodbye, tiny hairs and pet dander. Hello, shiny wood floor.

Am I spoiled? Sure. Am I addicted to the housekeeper? I can quit any time. Ultimately it comes down to happiness. And nothing makes me happy like crumb-free floors and shiny granite.

Glamorous Task

I START WITH A HOT CUP OF COFFEE AND TWO PIECES OF FUDGE. The drawer before me is a mess of tubs, tubes, and compacts, hair bands and hair—a chaos from which no beauty could emerge—unlike the pretty makeup on the counter, which is proudly displayed in leaded crystal and condescendingly mocks the dirty stepchildren shoved in the drawer.

As I dig into the mess I find I have enough black eyeliner—in different shades and degrees of sparkle—to survive the apocalypse. (You're not really asking if there are different shades of black, are you?)

I find five different colors of red lipstick, one of which I know to be at least ten years old. You can't just toss a red; you never know when you'll need one or another to mix just the right tint. Red matters. I spent years wearing a tangerine poppy shade after reading that while women prefer blue-toned reds, men are drawn to orange-based hues. Now, to brighten my task, I smear some scarlet on my lips. With the rest of my face bare, I am transformed into a forties movie star/harlot. Just as I'm thinking this look works better in black and white, my husband walks by and utters "Damn!" in a way that tells me the look is definitely more harlot than starlet. Not that there's anything wrong with that. Despite his—and most men's—declarations that they prefer a natural look, my husband has never complained about my made-up face, including the occasional overuse of apocalyptic eyeliner.

"Should I get the door?" he asks.

The thought of my children banging on our closed bedroom door is about as sexy as last spring's experiment with green eye shadow. Besides, while an organized makeup drawer may not rise to the level of "better than sex," if done right, it lasts longer. I politely decline.

My coffee has lost its steam so I indulge in the fudge as I pick through old foundation and a pot of glitter-something. I find a tube of Revlon Beyond Natural Primer. Beyond natural, way beyond—because it's actually plastic.

I don't understand the allure of primer, but beauty editors swear by the stuff so, since I've recovered it from the drawer of disorder, I vow to once again use the miracle elixir to spackle my pores. They're not so bad, as pores go, but also not so good that they couldn't use some silicone assistance. I smooth on the polymer, carefully avoiding my simmering red lips. Returning to the cosmetic confusion, I wonder why there are two of Step Two of my Mary Kay home micro-dermabrasion kit but only one of Step One.

Clearly I've been sanding at a faster rate than I've been replenishing.

I stop to play with an eyebrow kit because it's new, and because I am almost as obsessed with my eyebrows as I am with my lips. I throw away the toothbrush I ruined scrubbing the eye pencil sharpener. Then I toss the business card for the esthetician at the dermatologist's office, but only because her number is already programmed into my phone.

When I am done cleaning and culling, the drawer is organized into tidy compartments. I reward myself with the remaining fudge and admire my work. There is a container for everyday items: contact lenses, deodorant, makeup (like mascara) that's not pretty enough for the sink-side crystal tray. Another container holds sixteen shades of eye shadow. Yet another is home to a modest thirteen tubes of lipstick and gloss. (Don't worry, there are more throughout the house.) One final container holds resurfacing crystals and a micro-chemical peel. Floating free in the drawer are four more toothbrushes in case I need to tame an especially errant brow or clean all that waxy black eyeliner film from around the sink drain.

The coffee is cold, the fudge is gone, and my red lip shaped mark on the mug is the most glamorous residue of my task. I swipe a bit of ruby gloss over my crimson-stained lips. For the moment my world is in order. Which is a good thing, because my husband is back, eyeing me in the mirror.

This could get messy.

I Am the Wirus

FEW THINGS ARE MORE IMPORTANT TO A WRITER THAN A functional computer. Slow start-up, programs that close unexpectedly, and digital minions who save your words to a drive you've never heard of can cause any of us to channel our inner Hemingway. And I'm talking about his efficiency with liquor, not words. For bloggers, lack of a working gateway proves even more disastrous. We live to surf websites for opportunities, never knowing where we'll earn a quarter to write about our sock matching technique or a buck for our words about little Johnny's first bicuspid.

"Maybe it's not a virus," I told my husband. "Maybe it's Spyware." I liked pretending I knew what I was talking about.

"Spyware, huh?"

"Spies are everywhere," I said, looking around like a character in a cold war novel. I shrugged it off. "There must be something they can do right? I mean, don't you think they can fix it?"

"How can you get rid of it if it's spying on you?"

Smartass.

When I reached out for help, the men of a certain anti-virus protection outfit were only too happy to chat me up.

Ramesh: Welcome to the Antivirus Solution Center. How may I help you?

Lela: I have a problem with my web access. I think I have a virus, or spyware.

Ramesh: What is your 32-digit product number?

32-digit product number? This is exactly why I had put off contacting the virus people for over a month. If I had the kind of mind that could commit a 32-digit number to memory, I probably could have taken the computer apart and excised the electronic gremlin myself.

It took me a week to convince the chat guys that I had a legitimate problem, and it only happened then because during an online scan, the viral beast interrupted the scan. I was immediately upgraded from the chat service to a phone consult.

"Sounds like you have a wirus," my new helper announced.

Did he say walrus? "Pardon me?"

"I think you have a wirus."

Wirus? "No," I said. "My wireless is working fine."

"Not wireless, wi-rus." He sounded irritated.

Wirus, rirus… virus! "Yes, yes, I have a virus!"

May as well have been a walrus, because it was goo goo g'joobing all over my computer.

He transferred my case to the virus department, which he said would be in contact within forty-eight hours. Silly me, I thought the whole company was the virus department. I fought back bitterness. What's two more days when you've been dealing with an evil infection for over a month? If only hard drives responded to Monistat.

I tried to put the setback in perspective. I hesitate to write these words because some sinister program is probably watching as I type, but honestly, bad as it is, a computer virus is really not so bad, relatively speaking. Compared with real viruses, like Ebola or Bubonic plague, a computer worm is insignificant. I might miss a deadline, but no one's going to die if my laptop runs slow. No one's going to waste away if I can't check my email or trade a stock. No village will be flooded if I can't pay my gas bill on time.

A writing buddy recently described her falling out with a hard drive. "It was horrifying," she said.

Horrifying?

A strong word, even for writer who's had her words erased.

"I know," another writer commiserated. "I went through that last fall."

They nodded, touched hands, and their misery made me wonder if we need hospice for dying computers and grief counseling for lost manuscripts.

To be safe, guard against overconfidence around computers, especially if you're a writer. Think about it—the innocent looking Mac or PC knows our most private thoughts, to say nothing of the passwords to our bank accounts. They are spies, and they are everywhere.

Also, beware of mocking the chat room guys, even inside your head. As soon as I got the virus fixed, my wireless went out.

Portrait of a Junk Drawer

As A KID I ONCE OPENED THE WRONG DRAWER AT A FRIEND'S
house. Instead of the spoons her mother had asked for, I found
a broken ruler, chewed pencils, and a padlock splattered with
paint.

"Junk drawer," the mom said. "Everybody's got one."

What a relief. We had a drawer at home that held hair bands,
restaurant matches, and inkless pens. I'd assumed this was our
family's particular shame. Learning that other people suffered
the junk-sickness was comforting, but still, I wanted better for
myself. When I moved away from home, I tried not to repeat the
pattern, but somehow ended up maintaining my own junk
drawers in apartments and houses across the country. All the
while I dreamed of an organized space with cubbies for keys,
picture hanging hardware, and miniature screwdrivers.

I'm not quite there.

We have two junk drawers now: his and hers. His catches manly items like lighters, electrical tape, and the occasional nut and bolt. Mine is for the stuff of daily life. I open it no less than ten times a day and I organize it over and over in my continuous effort to get it to close properly.

First, I root out garbage because trash gives respectable junk drawers a bad name. I don't need an old church program or last May's third grade spelling list. I toss cardboard boxes and brochures for $45 bottles of acai berry juice. Of course, not all trash starts out as such, but is rendered useless over time. What good is $3 off a car wash in 2004? Was I planning to time travel? I find idea notes for stories scratched off on index cards: *Red Explorer-leaf pile playhouse-childhood dream with circus rat.* That's useful.

Some things inspire guilt, like my daughter's crumpled artwork. While my firstborn's early masterpieces hold a place of honor in a plastic tub somewhere, the second child will surely need art therapy later. There is the Scalpicin I bought before I realized the itchy scalp really was lice and not just some other irritant that, God forbid, the neighbors might mistake for lice. I debate where to put the telephone number to Poison Control (in case I splash nail polish remover in my daughter's eye again).

Then there are essentials. Sure, I can live without the nutritional information for McDonald's and Starbucks, but not my bent and faded Weight Watchers Points Counter. That stays. Also, Post-its, Sharpies, tape, and paper clips. These are must-have supplies in a well-stocked kitchen.

I finally reach the bottom of the drawer, only to find that uncapped pens have created inkblots that inspire me to peer deep into my psyche. Not good. The ink needs covering up—quick. Back into the drawer go immunization records, pencils, candy, scissors, and erasers. Back in for binder clips, thumb-tacks, and take-out menus.

Done. One little spot is relatively organized and I feel lighter. Though my drawer may not be perfect, it gets me through the day. And it shuts—for now.

Which is more than I can say for the silverware drawer.

Blacklisted

Mommy Meltdown

IT HAD BEEN ON THE CALENDAR FOR WEEKS: PIANO RECITAL—4 P.M. At 4:30, I realized we weren't there. I began a meltdown. The last time I'd experienced a guilt-fest that intense was Christmas Eve the year before when I'd been certain that I hadn't gotten my kids even one gift they wanted and worse yet, my wrapping sucked. Now, like then, I puddled onto my bedroom floor, sniffling and sobbing like a toddler. I'd failed as a mother yet again. I cried for the missed recital during broad daylight in front of the kids.

"Mom? Are you crying?" My daughter looked at me as if I'd grown an arm on top of my head.

"Are you okay?" my son was equally confused.

"I'm the worst mom ever," I blurted through the snot and tears. Not only would my children miss the chance to play the piano in front of all those adoring fans, but their names in the program would announce my failure.

Davidson. Davidson? Are you here? What's that—neither Davidson is here? Oh dear. It seems the Davidsons have other plans today.

Murmurs would float through the crowd. We'd be banned from the music school. Good mothers, afraid of my contagious badness, would move closer to each other when they saw me at Walmart. I'd be the Leper mom. My Good Mommy card would be revoked. And whose fault was that?

Mothers get no training, no license, no education credit hours to maintain. I screw up—a lot. For example, I once called my son a moron for spilling a box of angel hair pasta on the tile. No good mother would do that, but those noodles are hard to pick up, damn it. I've mastered the mommy apology: "Sorry, Sweetie. Mommy's very crabby today."

If only there were classes to teach us the intricacies of calendar management, lunch box basics, and play date etiquette. I want a certificate to hang on my wall, one I can point to and say, "This is what they taught me. I'm qualified." Maybe we can learn mothering by mail. Everything from pacifier maintenance to paying for college could be taught by correspondence courses and online chats.

Ambitious moms could go for an Associates Degree in Artsy Craftsy, or a Bachelors in Butt Wiping. Truly overachieving moms could go for their Masters in Mommy & Me or PhD in Potty Training. There would be continuous education in PTA management and extra credit for lice eradication. Face it, we need a curriculum. Women's intuition can leave a lot to chance.

As for the missed recital, it turned out there was another one the next day. By then my sobs had subsided and I watched with pride as my babies plunked out *Old MacDonald* and *Mary Had a Little Lamb* on the ivories. For this whisper of musical talent I had tiptoed at the edge of sanity. I obviously had much to learn.

While there may never be a formal training program for motherhood, we could all benefit from a few seminars, at least. Organizational skills, anyone? Or at the very least a workshop in how to cull a teachable moment from your Mommy Meltdown.

In the mean time, I'd advise you to buy a big calendar and a value pack of post-its. Consider these your Cliff's Notes.

The New Birthday Plan

DEAR SON,

I'm writing to tell you about an exciting change we'll be making in regard to birthdays this year!

Because this is a big birthday year for me (rhymes with shorty), and because you're such a big boy now, and frankly because I'm a little worn out with the whole kids' birthday scene, we're going to do things a little differently this year. Instead of me spending my time planning, executing, and cleaning up after your birthday party, you're going to do all that for my birthday.

Sounds like fun, right?

First you're going to help me make a list of all my very best friends. Don't worry, the guest list won't get out of hand. You know how I always limit the number of guests at your parties to your age? Same deal. I'll only be inviting forty friends. Because my friends are slightly geographically diverse, transporting them all to the party could be tricky. But you'll figure it out. Just like Daddy and I always find a way to shuttle your friends around. I promise my pals will smell better. Most of them, anyway.

Aren't you just dying to know the theme for my party? You know how you're always begging for pizza parties and laser tag parties and parties where you can eat pizza while riding go-carts and play laser tag in space? I want a cool party too. That's why I'll be going to a spa with my forty friends. (I have NO idea how much all this will cost, but you might want to start saving your allowance now.)

When you think about it, this spa idea is a pretty good deal for you because it frees you from cooking a bunch of food we might very well a) eat without tasting, b) throw at each other, or c) shove down our throats so fast it makes us sick enough to vomit on the good carpet.

After the party, of course I'll expect you to hound me night and day until I write each and every last thank you note. You'll also need to keep track of my gifts and write down exactly how to word my gratitude to each of my guests.

Finally, when I get bored will all my presents—like a week later—I'm going to be really crabby and whiny. I may refuse to do ordinary tasks like make your dinner and wash your underwear. Don't take this personally. After all, you're the one spoiling me rotten! I'm really excited about this year's birthday plans and so proud of you, my grownup little boy!

Love,
Mommy

Strategic Swearing

As we head into spring with our calendars carefully coordinated, piano lessons penned in next to sports practices and Pampered Chef parties, I occasionally want to cuss. It is sometimes wise, and when used in the proper context, swearing—especially to, or at, our children—can be highly motivating.

I'm a Hockey Mom, which means I sit in the stands yelling, "GO-GO-GO!" and "GET THE PUCK!" as if I have half a clue what I'm talking about. I have also been known to scream, "KEEP YOUR STICK DOWN!" during particularly lively games—though I have no idea why that's important. Being a Hockey Mom also means I've got to get my kids dressed in a ton of gear while they wiggle and complain and high-five their friends. I may use a little foul language when I lace the skates, but that is the hushed, hope-the-other-parents-don't-hear kind of swearing. It's not strategic.

For all the effort I put into the sport, I want my son to care.

Months of nagging and pleading to get dressed faster, skate harder, and go after the puck had proved unsuccessful. It was his third year playing and he just didn't seem to enjoy it—until I asked if he wanted to play in the tournament that's five hours and $500 away. Suddenly he's interested. Anything to swim in a hotel pool.

He seemed to respond to my husband's pep talks, so one night at practice I decided to try a pep talk of my own. I kept the mothering to a minimum and tried to conjure motivating sports talk as I got him dressed.

Nothing. The combination of his apathy and my determination not to point it out made me want to drop an F-Bomb. Thankfully, my frustration led to my epiphany. I didn't know sports, but I knew how to punctuate a sentence. Just before my son put on his helmet, I grasped his shoulders, looked him in the eyes and said,

"Listen to me."

He looked at me with that bored, "Yeah-what?" expression.

"I want you to go out there—" I lowered my head and looked out over my glasses, "—and kick some ASS!"

His eyes almost popped out.

"I know," I said. "And no, you're not allowed to say that, but I am."

His surprise turned to determination. The kid moved like I've never seen. He strapped his helmet in an instant, hit the ice with a fury, smacked his stick against the puck and nearly scored a goal. Nothing sparks maternal pride like an ass-kicker. It made me wonder what other situations might benefit from a little strategic swearing.

Clean up your f***ing room!

Eat the g** d*** mushroom!

Get your s**t off the yard!

I started thinking this could work. Of course, it would be a fine line to walk. I wouldn't want the kid so desensitized that my cursing would lose its power. It could take time to learn to pepper in the profanity just right—strategically, but it would be worth it.

And to hell with good parenting. The kid's going to learn to swear somewhere. May as well come from a pro.

Got Stuff?

I'VE LIVED FOR YEARS IN VARIOUS PLACES WITHOUT GOOD SHOPPING, which is fine. My life offers few occasions too good for an outfit from The Gap. However, the idea of a new mall made me giddy. Sure, there was the shopping, but malls are also about bringing people together. Or maybe just about gathering them all in one place so they can shop for stuff. Maybe I was slightly concerned that with a shiny new mall so close to home I could put a dent in the budget. Still, how could I resist the lure of open-air browsing, high-end stores, and piped-in sound? I had to make peace with the new mall—meet it head on and conquer my urge to splurge.

I dressed up for its brand-new-ness, needing to look good to bolster myself against the temptation of all that glossy stuff calling my name. I took my kids to make sure I wouldn't stay too long. The place had it all, clean as Disneyland, bright and new. From my small town vantage point, it was a lifeline to Someplace Else with spots for people to congregate, and Big City stores.

I drooled for Haagen Daz, but refused to pay $3 a scoop. Reasoning that my kids wouldn't know the difference, we headed to the Dairy Queen, housed in an extraordinary food court. Next to the bright plastic tables and chairs was the lounge, where shoppers' uninterested entourages relaxed on clean, upholstered furniture watching plasma screens mounted over a stone hearth. I wondered how dingy and disgusting the comfy chairs would look after a year's worth of old-man-head and teenage musk settled in.

After the ice cream, we braved the stores. I reminded myself that I had all I needed at home, but still, there were those boots, the crystal goblets, the fluffy blankets. I prevailed. When we left the stores for the energy of the crowd, I realized that's what I really missed about the city anyway. It wasn't the stuff, but all those people.

My kids begged to go to Build-A-Bear, but we negotiated instead for a children's clothing store. I was at first delighted, then dismayed to find there were racks of clothes that both my daughter and I could fit into. We could be matching! Charming, yet I couldn't help feeling sorry for the overfed ten-year-old who wears my size.

My son tried on a black velour sport coat, which the mannequin wore over an un-tucked button-down shirt with a loosened tie. It was cute in the way that old pictures of a wasted twelve-year-old Drew Barrymore at Studio 54 are cute. He looked like a young Colin Farrell—minus the stubble. No purchase there.

My feet ached, and after another twenty minutes of navigating the crowd, all those people started to wear me out.

I bought one thing: an amazing raspberry chipotle sauce we used to buy in Texas. For the life of me I couldn't remember what we put it on, but we used to buy it by the barrel so I shelled out $10 for an eight-ounce bottle. I swung that little bag of very-special-sauce to the bounce in my step.

I had succeeded! I'd resisted the lure of all things sparkly and smelling of newness. I proved that I could go to the mall and enjoy the sights, the people, the colored water fountain, and the smooth-but-still-cool-jazz floating through the cool evening air without going home burdened by a bunch of junk I didn't need.

Good for me.

Now groceries, that's another story. There's bliss in the aisles of a Sam's Club—and you don't even have to dress up.

Best Mom Ever: School Counselor

ON THE WAY TO SCHOOL ONE MORNING MY DAUGHTER WAS CLOSE
to tears. "What's wrong?" I asked. Turns out her oh-so-sensi-
tive brother had made an appointment for them to visit the
school counselor.

"We fight all the time," he explained. "It's a problem and we
need to solve it."

"But I didn't DO anything," my daughter whined.

"Don't worry, Sweetie," I said. "You're not in trouble."

"But I didn't do ANYTHING!" Drops pooled in her eyes.

It occurred to me that if my son insisted on psychological intervention, I could give it to him. I've watched Dr. Phil. How hard
could it be? Besides, I wanted the juicy details that drove him
to seek professional help.

At breakfast the next day I played counselor.

"So what would you like to talk about?" I asked.

My son answered while my daughter averted her eyes.

"Well, we fight," he said. "Real bad."

My daughter folded her arms and clenched her jaw.

"Mm-hmm. And how does that make you feel?" I asked.

"Bad," said the boy.

"Bad," said the girl.

"Okay. So, you fight and that makes you both feel bad. Is that right?"

They both nodded.

"What do you fight about?" They were both quiet for a minute, then looked at each other.

My daughter spoke up. "Sometimes we play games and he always makes up the powers and he gives himself all the good powers."

I shook my head. It always comes down to power.

"Is this true?" I turned to my son. "Do you repeatedly endow yourself with the superior super powers?"

"Yes," he said, hanging his head.

"How does that make you feel?" I asked my daughter.

"It sort of makes me feel not listened to."

"Okay." Trying to keep a straight face, I turned to my son. "Did you know you taking all the good powers made your sister feel not listened to?"

"Yeah."

"And how does that make you feel?"

"Bad."

By this time I was starting to feel my own super powers. I'm more of a figure-it-out-yourself kind of Mom, but this babble seemed to be working.

"So what do you think you guys could do so that you don't fight so much?"

"Maybe we could make up the games together?" said the girl.

"That might work," said the boy.

"How would that make you feel if you two didn't fight anymore?"

"That would feel good," they said together with great exhalations of relief.

Not too shabby Dr. Davidson. I smiled, triumphant. "Now you don't need to go see the counselor."

The Boy's eyes popped open wide, then narrowed.

"Yes we do." His brows knotted.

"Why? We already solved the problem."

"Because, Mom, you're not the real counselor."

At least I got my daughter off the hook. When he finally visited the counselor at school, he went alone.

"So what did she say?" I was dying to know.

"She thought you had some pretty good ideas."

Ha! Once again, I missed my calling. "So I'm not a total loser?"

"No, Mom," he said. "You're the Best Mom Ever."

"Really?"

"Sure."

And that's how I learned that sarcasm is genetic.

26 Ways to Torture Children

THIS IS A STORY OF REVENGE. BEFORE SCHOOL LET OUT IN THE spring, my son's class was assigned to write an ABC book. They could choose any topic they wanted as long as they came up with 26 things. My dear son decided to write 26 Ways to Annoy Your Mom. I had to get him back. There are many, many more, but here are my favorite 26 Ways to Torture Children.

A – Always serve spinach, occasionally with a side of mushrooms.

B – Beat them with a stick. Not hard, just enough to get their attention.

C – Cuddle them in public. Singing a favorite lullaby also works well.

D – Drone on about how totally rad the 80s were. Like, they, like, totally were.

E – Eat the last cupcake. Also, lick the frosting off their cupcakes. They hate that.

F – Fail to wash their soccer socks three times a week.

G – Gush over their dimples when their friends come by.

H – Hug your spouse and call him or her Babe.

I – Invite the boy or girl who they like over, and cue up Barry White.

J – Just say no to Poptarts.

K – Kiss hello at soccer practice.

L – Limit Nintendo DS use to times when it is convenient for you.

M – Move the chips to the top shelf.

N – Never give extra chocolate sauce.

O – Order broccoli as a replacement for fries.

P – Punish them with chores. Start with poop-scooping.

Q – Quit buying bread that that is softer than your pillow.

R – Remind them to pick up their rooms. Again.

S – Sing along to the radio during carpool.

T – Talk about puberty in front of the opposite sex.

U – Underestimate how long it'll take if they come grocery shopping with you.

V – Voice your concern for their safety. Over, and over, and over, and over…

W – Withhold allowance.

X – Xerox their baby pictures and decoupage them on their lunch boxes.

Y – Yodel.

Z – Zing them with retaliatory comments in a public forum.

Fear the Bunny

Every year my kids choose Halloween costumes. And every year since they were about four they have insisted that those costumes be different than the ones they wore the year before. As if anyone remembers. But okay.

Off we go to Walmart to find something good. Wait a minute—what am I saying? We don't do that at all. Turns out I'm WAY too cheap to spend $20 each and every year for some half-sewn wad of polyester. No, it's a rare day that we buy off-the-shelf goblin attire. Usually I send my children into the closet with a pair of blunt scissors and a Sharpie.

"Be creative," I say. And they are.

One year my son made a convincing Luke Skywalker outfit from nothing but a scrap of burlap and the core from an old roll of wrapping paper. My daughter looked just like Laura Ingalls Wilder in a dress made from pillowcases and strategically placed potholders. They have paraded the neighborhood as fairies, witches, ghosts, and pirates. All without resorting to the Halloween aisle. But last year my girl settled on her dream costume long before we ventured into the closet.

"I want to be a bunny rabbit," she told me. Great, I thought. I started mentally planning: white t-shirt, blush pink nose, floppy rag ears, done. I was all for it until she added, "We can use ketchup for the blood."

I hadn't factored in the blood.

It soon became clear that my daughter didn't want to be an ordinary bunny, but an evil bunny rabbit—the one from Monty Python. She wanted to be the bunny with the vicious teeth. If you haven't seen the Holy Grail, you'll find this all a bit demented. You see, there's a bunny, lots of blood, and an injured knight of the round table. (All very family friendly I assure you.)

Although I'd rather she dress up as something a little less menacing, my daughter was intent on being evil. Who knew my cute second grader was a Halloween purist? I can't blame her. Halloween is supposed to be scary. It's fun to play evil. Who would you rather pretend to be—Cruella DeVille or the lame chick trying to save the puppies? Playing evil is fun because it's make-believe. And we all know that real evil doesn't wear vampire teeth.

In the end, I was able to talk my angel of a girl into being a green-faced witch. She got to be scary, but traditional too, and in my opinion, sweet and nostalgic.

This year she told me she wants to be a hot dog. So apparently she's simply intent on splashing herself with ketchup. And she knows how to work the system.

Seven Surefire Ways to Get Blacklisted from the PTA

YOU HATE THE PTA. ADMIT IT. YOU'D RATHER CLEAN OUT THE drain than volunteer for field day or bake muffins for all those ungrateful teachers. But someone's got to do it, right? Much as you cannot stand the thought of one more silent auction, you don't want to be that mom—the slacker who doesn't care enough about the social and educational future of her children to get her lazy ass down to the cafeteria for the float committee meeting.

Instead of actually having to say no, wouldn't it be easier to get kicked right out of the PTA? Now you can. I can help. Here are seven surefire techniques for getting banned from the PTA forever:

#1 – Pass out peanuts.

Peanuts in public schools are like anthrax in Washington, D.C. Distribute peanut M&Ms to the kids in your charge at the petting zoo and you'll never be asked to organize another field trip.

#2 – Get a job.

This is a drastic step, but if you miss enough of those 10 a.m. meetings, you'll never be asked to join another committee. The beauty of this technique is that to be successful you don't actually have to get a job, but merely convince others that you have.

#3 – Botch the bulletin board.

You will eventually be asked to create an adorable science-themed bulletin board made of Q-Tips, or a stunning botanical scene for the second grade musical created entirely of peat moss. If you're in a hurry to get the boot, volunteer for this. It's just so easy to make something horrid.

#4 – Show off your tramp stamp.

There is nothing to get mouths a-gaping like a little ink below the waistline. Strategic use of low-rise jeans can insulate you from years of Fall Carnival shifts, spaghetti socials, and any other event that would put you in proximity of any Mr. PTAs.

#5 – Buy the wrong color.

It doesn't matter what it is—balloons, paper plates, napkins— go against the committee's ruling on a particular nuance of forest green and you can kiss your PTA career goodbye.

#6 – Piss off the Queen.

Work with your personality to find the most effective way to enrage the PTA Queen. It's important to understand that PTA Queens often operate outside the official hierarchy of the PTA system. Learn who they are, irritate them, and go on with your merry non-PTA existence.

#7 – Embezzle the funds.

This is perhaps the most drastic step of all, but in many cases can result not only in your being shunned from the PTA, but every other well-meaning, time-sucking volunteer organization in town.

Keep all these in mind next time you stroll your happy little self down to the PTA meeting. Because really, aren't they all a little easier than just saying no?

Texting: Make Mine Unlimited

A LOT OF THINGS ARE DIFFERENT FOR OUR KIDS THAN THEY WERE for us. We didn't have home theaters, decent video games, or twenty-four-seven kids' television programming. But the thing that's really changed everything is cell phones and the privacy they offer our children . Before my son started middle school I had made up my mind that I would not cave to the pressure.

"You'll change your tune," a friend told me. "What if he misses the bus?" she questioned. I rolled my eyes.

Cut to Christmas and my son tearing open a cell phone while his little sister calculates the number of months she has to wait for hers under the "big-brother-broke-them-in" algorithm. I'm still not convinced he needs a phone, but he wanted one and it was Christmas.

I was weak. Or maybe noble, triumphing over my jealousy. Having a personal phone—not to mention a modest texting allowance—in the 6th grade? I never had it so good.

Back in the olden days we didn't even have cordless phones. Telephones were all attached to a wall, either in your home or in public. You carried a quarter for a payphone and everyone could see you cry when your mom forgot to pick you up from soccer practice. If you missed the bus you didn't call anyone; you walked home. When you got sick at school you had to use the office phone with its rotary dial and plastic cubes across the bottom. To have a private conversation at home you stretched the phone cord down that hall, pinching it in your bedroom door, then prayed your mom wouldn't detach it from the wall while you were asking your BFF if she wanted to "go with" the new boy (who was named Curt or Tyler or Rob). Those deliriously fortunate enough to have a phone in their rooms knew their parents were listening in from the kitchen.

Today's kids don't have to worry about parents overhearing conversations, partly because phones are rarely used for speaking to one another anymore. The important information—what band is cool, whose house they're sleeping over at, and which color Converse to wear tomorrow—is all relayed via text. It goes without saying that back in the olden days we didn't have our own secret language that our parents couldn't figure out. We had to be clever and make plans while they weren't listening or watching.

Whatever, Dad—no, you did not know we were sneaking out the sliding glass door!

Now kids speak in an ever-evolving code of letters and symbols—ikr? It's a miracle our olden days thumbs didn't fall off like the vestigial tail from lack of use.

Popular as texting has become, I still thought my 11-year-old son was too young for it. I figured he just used the phone as a status symbol and to call me on the [many] days I forgot it was my turn at carpool. I didn't realize he was using the text function at all until I started using it on my own phone. When my texts racked up I worried about the potential overage costs so I logged into my account. While I was slightly under my plan limit of two hundred texts, my son was up to eight hundred twenty—two weeks into the billing cycle. I immediately called my provider to request unlimited texting.

I sensed a golden opportunity. His excess was just what I needed to institute the partial pay policy I should have started when we gave him the phone. I confronted him with the facts.

"But, Mom," he almost cried, "it's not like you can just end a conversation."

Awww… proof that my baby boy is not yet a man.

I told him that instead of making him pay for the overage, he was going to chip in ten dollars a month toward his phone bill.

"But then I'll have less money," he whined.

I didn't laugh. I did however take my platinum opportunity to ask for his phone, and read his texts. If I were a terrible person I would transcribe them here, because they would make you laugh and reminisce over everything that was good and true and hasn't changed about the summer before 7th grade.

But I won't.

Because I am a good mother and because I'm beyond grateful for what I read there, in his private conversations with friends, both boys and girls. For now, for today—though he doesn't realize it—my baby is as innocent as the day I brought him home wrapped in flannel and smelling like spit-up.

If only there were an unlimited plan for that.

Happily Ever After

Chasing Date Night

AFTER ELEVEN YEARS, TWO KIDS, AND EVERY RERUN OF LAW AND Order, it had come to this: Date Night. Don't pretend you don't know what I'm talking about. It's supposed to make us better, stronger, more romantic. Chasing that illusion, I painted my eyes like an Arabian princess and lured my husband away from familiar platters of cow-and-tater with a wink and a promise. We hit the highway. Away from PTA, soccer, and the backyard BBQs of our tidy subdivision.

I tasted youth. It tasted a lot like lip gloss.

In the university district, a bistro beckoned. Blue neon 'Jazz' lit up the window. Even better: convenient parking.

As we waited for our table, I admired our reflections behind the bartender. Totally still hot. The hostess led us past the Beautiful People with their tiny bowls of pasta to a small stairway. Ooh, what now? A lower level? Not only had we found the hippest spot in town, we were now being shown into its inner sanctum. Date

Night rocked.

The grotto grooved a different vibe. Retro, with booths, hoola-dancer lamps, and pop-art. Very Bradys-go-to-Vegas.

"Good choice, gorgeous," my husband said. But as I waited an unreasonable interval for my Chardonnay, I missed the candle-light upstairs. How soon would all the eye paint settle into my not-so-fine lines? Once the wine arrived, I tried to pretend it didn't taste like yesterday's tea. The soup had to be better—Cream of Asparagus and Crab could be nothing less than divine.

"Do you notice anything about the people down here?" I asked.

"No," my husband lied. But everyone around us sported thicker waists and thinner hair.

"I think this is the *Old People* section," I whispered.

"Nah."

As I forced myself through cold, starchy soup, springs dug into my motherly rear. I poked at mediocre shrimp and soggy salad. Date Night evaporated like a mirage. Not having spent time on eye make-up, my husband was less vexed.

"This place might not last long," he said.

"It's crap," I said. The whole place looked like a yard sale that had been plowed over by a wood-paneled station wagon. This basement sucked.

Just then, a Cowboy and his Girl moseyed in. Neither *Old* nor *Beautiful*, and worlds away from cool, they cleared things up. We had been banished. Not to be seen by the real clientele. Hidden away like a cousin with Herpes at the church picnic.

And me with my best mascara.

I knew complaints wouldn't earn me a place upstairs. But such a severe humiliation required resolution. I needed chocolate.

At the steakhouse a friendly waitress promptly served us a fudgy cake-frosting-sauce concoction, which delivered more than it promised. As our cheeks blushed under the light of a Budweiser sign, we found the satisfaction that had eluded us all evening.

So maybe we should start at the steakhouse? Nah. After all, dating is all about the chase.

Busted

At my kids' recent physical, the doctor busted me.

"Anyone in the house smoke?"

"No," I said, totally telling the truth.

"Mom," my daughter said. She looked at me wide-eyed as if I'd said a bad word. Then she turned from me to her new role model, the kind and presumably honest doctor.

"My dad smokes," she said.

"Busted!" said the doctor.

Cut to me backpedaling and using way too many words to explain away my husband's weekly cigar. Or was it nightly? Either way, he smoked outside so it didn't really count, right?

"Right," the doctor assured. She was nice, unlike the little traitor I'd been feeding for half a decade.

That brush with not-even-bad behavior made me want to let out a rebel yell. Being a grown up can be so lame. We're not allowed to do anything!

Last summer I got busted at a friend's backyard pool party.

By the time the cops showed up, we had dwindled to a dozen thirty-somethings around a half empty keg making really bad karaoke. (Back in the day, I rocked a pretty hard Love Shack baby, but that involved way more alcohol than my adult liver cares to process.) There I was, having fun in a mature and non-rebellious way, drinking beer not purchased by anyone's older sister or boyfriend, but by the tax-paying homeowner himself. We'd already gathered up our bags and started goodbyes when two young officers appeared inside the gate. I would have sworn they were strippers. Either that or our host put them up to it to make us all feel younger and badder. But they were totally serious. After interrupting a particularly heartbreaking rendition of Prince's "Kiss," they said to the homeowners—and I quote—"Don't make us come back out here."

Had someone been watching *Cops*? I was dying for the DJ to cue up that Bad Boys song. *What-chou gonna do? What-chou gonna do when they come for you?* The guy who'd had to stop mid-Falsetto looked like my eight-year-old when I say lights out: Just a little longer? Pleeeeze!

I wondered what the officers expected to find. No criminals here. Just a bunch of adults with too many mayonnaise-based salads and a beer fridge full of milk.

My husband, who hadn't been too hot on the party idea, gave me a look that said this never happens while watching *World's Greatest Engineering Feats*. But we'd had a great time. Who can argue with burgers, brew and 'tater salad? The only thing missing were his cigars.

The big question—other than, don't the police have some Meth labs to eradicate?—was who would call the cops on us? Did the shrill of our under-primed voices at 10:15 on a Saturday night rile the neighbors? Was backyard karaoke now a crime? Bad words crowded the tip of my well-behaved, un-pierced tongue.

Wary of the fuzz and their dreaded breathalyzers, we retreated, sharing stories from Fondmemoryland where life was one big kegger. We recalled busts long past and embellished tales of daring escapes and stealth camouflage in basements and shrubberies.

I accept that booze must now be tempered with chips and dips, that the babysitter needs to be home by eleven, and that I really shouldn't swear in front of the children, but can't we have any fun at all? On the drive home I wondered if the OnStar people could fine me for singing off key to the radio.

I wanted to be irked about the cops showing up to ruin our fun, but truth was, the party was pretty much over by the time they showed up and nothing can make you feel like your old rebel self like getting busted by the cops. Even if it was only for really bad singing.

Used To Be

REMEMBER HOW IT USED TO BE WHEN YOU WERE YOUNG AND YOU had no responsibilities? Life was one big party and your biggest dilemma was who to hook up with at the end of the evening?

I do, barely.

My husband had been working in Mexico, and going on and on about this fabulous place he'd been going to with the people from work—the young people. You can imagine my excitement.

"It's great," he said. "You start out eating at these long tables and then slowly the music gets louder and louder and pretty soon everybody's dancing!"

I remember dancing. But contrary to the way my husband portrayed himself during our courting phase, he's no dancer. It's not that he doesn't want to dance. A severe lack of rhythm prevents him from doing so. When we were young it didn't matter. We used to be the life of the party, dancing on speakers and deep dipping. But now—well, all that used-to-be went out the window with the I-Do's, the real jobs, and the flannel packets of baby.

Except that now my husband is out dancing again.

"That's nice," I told him. "I'd do the same if I weren't busy cleaning sand out of your children's hair."

"It's a cultural thing," he said.

"I've also been keeping the mildew at bay."

"It's a different life down there." Wistfully, he gazed out the window. While I may have a touch of used-to-be syndrome, my husband suffers from a bad case of somewhere-else-is-better. He's never accepted that life is different when you're just visiting. No place is one big party all the time. Eventually the alarm clock rings and everybody goes to work.

I'm not the only one who likes to reminisce. I called a friend recently to wish her a happy birthday. It's been 15 years since we lit up the town, but we remember.

Remember that one time? We were so drunk....

Didn't you flash a cop?

Was that the night someone puked off the porch?

Who was that anyway?

LELA DAVIDSON

Good times.

Good times.

Last fall I went to a bar for girls' night out with some friends.
Half the "girls" couldn't make it because of sick kids and work
deadlines, but the rest of us set off to see a live band in a bar. We
stepped back in time, into a place where you emerge at the end
of the evening with no voice and reeking of smoke. Too many
bodies pressed up against each other sucked up all the oxygen.
Third world countries had better bathrooms.

After a long wait in line, I made my way through the crowd with
a beer in each hand. A friend looked at me funny. "What?" I
said. Just because I hadn't been in a bar in a while didn't mean
I'd forgotten everything. "I'm not waiting in that line again."

The band made me feel old and law-abiding. Maybe I've gotten
really square in my maternal bliss, but since when do bands play
two full sets of songs about smoking pot? The boys from Oklahoma roll their joints too long. Who knew?

"You could have warned me about that band," I said to a PTA
mom the next week at the 1st grade musical.

"What band?"

"Cross Canadian Ragweed."

She stopped messing with her camera long enough to give me a
look.

"They have the word weed in their name!" she said. "What did you expect?"

That's just it. I don't know what to expect anymore. With teenagers in my future, I've decided it's important to go into a bar at least once a year—to keep informed. Purely research. And I mean a real bar, not one of those smooth jazz playing joints that sell booze to old people.

In the meantime I decided to mosey down to Mexico and check out this restaurant my husband had been raving about. We ate and drank beer and hung out with his young colleagues. The music got louder and dance videos appeared on the stucco walls. Chairs were flung backwards to make room for the dancing. It was not so much a cultural experience as a bar with a lot of other people living out our used-to-be.

And there we were. Me about to die from smoke inhalation and beer bloat, and my faithful husband standing by, bottle in hand, nodding his head back and forth like a rhythm-less turkey.

Goodbye used-to-be; welcome to here and now.

Top Ten Reasons to Date Your Spouse
This Year

I COULD SPEND ALL WEEK COMING UP WITH VALID REASONS NOT TO spend precious time engaged in some artificially romantic date night. But the truth is we need them. Here are the top ten reasons why.

10. Dating is cheaper than couples counseling—not to mention divorce.

Every relationship requires maintenance. Seeing a movie or taking a walk with your spouse is much less expensive (and more fun) than twice weekly sessions on an outdated sofa in on a counselor's office. Date night costs a fraction of what you'd spend from your side of a well-apportioned attorney's desk. Think of these expenditures as an investment not only in your happiness, but in your long-term financial health as well.

9. Your spouse is hotter than you think.

We all get tired of looking at our partners. No matter how much they set us a flutter in the beginning, the sparkle wears off. Sometimes (admit it) you check out other people's spouses and think, "Dang! That's a hot one!" Rest assured that while you are mid-melt, someone else is checking out your own partner. It's nothing to be ashamed of, just human nature. Date night—especially if you both take the time to shave in the right spots—can remind you what you saw in this person in the first place—because for most people, it had at least a little to do with a hotness factor.

8. Date night is a guilt-free way to get away from your kids.

Do you enjoy spending every minute with your kids? Again, you don't have to raise your hand in public, but be honest. The extreme urge to get very far away from the creatures you birthed is natural. We all need adult time. Unfortunately, the guilt that comes along with that desire is common. Date nights are the exception because you know that taking care of your relationship is one of the single most important things you can do for your children's overall well-being. You know that, right?

7. You used to be really into each other.

Between the diapers, the [oops] late electric bill, and that odd smell in the hallway, romance can get away from you—quick. Sometimes sitting on the couch (after having just spent twenty minutes vying for the remote) you wonder how you ended up with this person. Getting away from everything together helps you focus on each other—on what attracted you (besides the, um, heat.) You may be surprised to find you're still kind of into each other—at least until you need to get home to unclog the drain.

6. There is no Bravo vs. Discovery Channel on a date.

We all get selfish. When the routine at home gets stressful, we seek comforts, from eating the foods we like to watching what we want on TV. All of these petty preferences divide us. The great thing about date night is it has an agenda. Even if you're only going to a coffee shop to share a triple-choco-latte, you're there to be together. That's the only objective. It's not about what you want or what your partner wants, the time has been set aside to spend time together as a unit.

5. Shoes, shoes, shoes.

When you have young kids you can start to feel frumpy fast. If you don't have a date night, what excuse have you got to dress up? Some of us end up covered in spit-up most days. Even if you dress in "real clothes" for work every day, you still need the glamour date night provides. Couples need to see each other at top form once in a while (see above). And it's fun. Remember, you don't have to spend a lot of money to look cute. (But if you've got a little extra, I'd spend it on shoes.)

4. The kids love eating mac-n-cheese out of a box.

Your kids will enjoy seeing their parents go out and do something fun. They might not admit it, and they may even try to pour on a little guilt, but it can only do them good to see mom and dad make each other a priority. You'll be setting a good example, and they really do like that junky food we fix on our way out to something better. (Oh, STOP feeling guilty. It's not every night!)

3. It may be the only night of the month you actually do your hair.

Seriously, hair can take a long time! The point here is not that you're not already bathing on a regular basis, but that everyone needs special things to look forward to. Sometimes our regular work-a-day and take-care-of-the-kids lives don't offer many opportunities to shine. Maybe you aren't working your dream job or slicing your carrots on granite countertops, but you can make date night a bright spot on your calendar.

2. Date night is a good time to reminisce.

In the early years of a relationship friends are always asking how you met. This inevitably leads to sweet or funny or mushy stories of eyes locking and hands trembling and blahty-blah-blah-blah. But it's fun, and reminds you why you (see above) a) find each other hot, and b)used to be quite into each other. So live a little, in the past. You don't want rely memories for all your contentment because that would mean you're not busy making new memories, but reminiscing about any good times together (not just at the beginning) is good for your future.

And the number one reason to date your spouse:

1. It could lead to sex.

Sex is really, really good for you. You need it. Just like food and water, it's fundamental to good health—both your physical well-being and that of your relationship. Obviously, date night is critical. How do you expect to get naked with someone you can't have a conversation with? A scheduled date night is not the be-all-end-all solution to every relationship trouble, but it's one little thing you can do. And it's not the grand gestures define a relationship; it's the little things, added up over time, that fortify. So think little, as in—get a little.

Date Night Etiquette

BECAUSE THINGS TEND TO GET A LITTLE—LET'S SAY RELAXED—
with a long time partner, many couples commit to a date night.
Before you do, consider a refresher course in dating etiquette.
Here are some Do's and Don'ts to keep in mind for successful
dating.

DO make an effort to look your best. The shorts you wore to
garden or mow the lawn are not appropriate date night attire,
no matter how comfortable.

DON'T point out the dieter's special on the menu. Eating light
on a date is one thing; suggesting it to your date is reserved for
the pre-committed relationship phase.

DO shave if you need to. This is a hard and fast dating rule and
it doesn't matter that you already did it once today. Do it again.

DON'T ask if you're getting lucky tonight. If you are, you'll know soon enough. If not, you've now ruined your chances for next time, too.

DO talk about something besides your pets and/or children. Your spouse is not nearly as interested in them as you think. Ditto for your boring job.

DON'T keep checking Facebook or the score on whatever game you're missing. You will be back to your pathetic existence-as-usual soon enough. Enjoy the moment you're actually in.

DO give each other some privacy to get ready. There's nothing that spoils the mood so much as your date watching you tame the rogue eyebrow.

DON'T accept any old excuse to skip date night. The dog's toenails can be clipped tomorrow. In fact, those suckers can go for months.

DO build up the excitement with some pre-date flirtation. If you don't know how to sext, just ask that high school kid next door.

DON'T flirt with the waiter or waitress. And don't act like you don't know what I'm talking about.

There you are—refreshed and completely primed for your next adventure in dating. And one last don't: if you don't follow my advice, don't say I didn't warn you!

How to Date Like a President

THE PRESIDENT AND FIRST LADY HAVE MADE IT PUBLIC THAT THEY embrace date night. If the leader of the most powerful nation on Earth, responsible for maintaining world peace and keeping the markets from spiraling ever downward, can commit to a regular date night, what's stopping you? Sure, the Obamas have more than their share of reasons to skip date night, but let's not overlook their advantages. Despite all the responsibilities facing the First Couple, they have a few things going for them:

⤳ The Obamas have live-in help. Even if the First Family didn't include Michelle's mother, I'm pretty sure they'd have a hook-up for quality childcare on demand. ~ You have that girl down the street who just started to drive and wear black eyeliner. If you're lucky and call three weeks ahead, she's available.

⤳ The Obamas have a limo and driver, which leaves little chance of getting in a fight on the way to the restaurant because Barack won't stop to ask for directions. ~ You have a minivan with Chick-Fil-A ground into the seats and a collection of pinecones from the state park rolling around the back. Sexy.

⤳ The Obamas have lots of invitations to parties and events. I'm pretty sure they're not sitting around on Thursday night trying to decide how to spice up their date night. ~ You live in the suburbs where on any given date night you might be choosing between Red Lobster, a pottery class, and a talk on that endangered bird.

⤳ The Obamas possess the hotness factor. Face it: we'd all be more excited if our mates were as toned and attractive as Barack and Michelle. ~ You squeeze fitness in between trips to the new Target and dance recitals, and your personal beauty routine consists of flossing.

⤳ The Obamas have less time together. The demands of the presidency make it that much more important for them to carve out quality time together. ~ You spend way too much time with your spouse as it is. All you want to do on the weekend is escape. Besides, isn't cleaning the garage quality time enough?

First Lady Michelle Obama stated in an interview that her big moment of realization of just how important date night really is came when one of their daughters mentioned how much she loved seeing her parents hold hands and go out on a date. Remember that next time you feel selfish leaving the kids behind. Call me, I'll come over for Secret Service duty.

Hot Date at Sam's Club

I WRITE A COLUMN GIVING ADVICE ABOUT HOW TO HAVE ROMANTIC date nights with your spouse. I've encouraged married folk to commit to a regular date night, shake things up with novel activities, and take that extra time to prepare for and flirt with their spouses. I've profiled happily married couples and even created a primer on how to date like the Obamas.

I'm such a fraud.

My own dating life is not so healthy. My dates lack the romantic spark I advocate. On a recent Saturday night, for example, my husband and I experienced the rare thrill of being childless for a few hours. I sat on his lap and told him there was something I wanted to do. Before he even had time to ponder the possibilities, I laid it on him: what I really, really wanted—was Sam's Club.

I wasn't lured by the flattering fluorescent lighting or the possibility of making out in a pleather recliner in the furniture aisle.

No, I needed to scope out the food options for the fortieth birthday party I was throwing myself. (In more romantic couples, the person not actually having the big milestone birthday might be the one to plan the party, but this is about us.)

Let the dating begin!

First we stopped at the optical counter, where I talked John into some stylish new frames. A few minutes later we shared samples of Goldfish crackers and compared the price of meat and cheese trays. He told me he'd take care of everything for the party, which is not how it will work, but it sounded nice, and saying pretty things is half of romance.

A particularly zesty looking tray of enchiladas wouldn't let us go. We picked them up to pop into the microwave at home. Our hot date would now include a romantic meal. The free appetizer course was served in store: pizza, granola bars, and sausage.

We saw and were seen. Among the thirty-pound bags of avocados and lifetime supplies of Pop Tarts, we found people we knew—a neighbor, a friend, a co-worker. Turned out Sam's was the place to be that Saturday night.

We even held hands.

There were no cute jeans, no sexy shoes. I didn't blow out my hair or retouch my makeup. But it was nice. This errand I could have done on my own was as good a date as any. Doing it together reminded me of how life used to be before the business end of our family got so big it required dividing up all the little tasks that used to bring us together.

We went home and shared those enchiladas in the living room like old times. John tried to sit next to me on the love seat, but it wasn't comfortable and we've got nothing to prove. He headed over to the recliner, where I was welcome to join him for a make out session—or not. And he let me pick the movie.

Maybe I'm not such a fraud after all.

Retiring Romance

RECENTLY MY HUSBAND AND I SAT DOWN WITH A RETIREMENT specialist to discuss our financial future. I am the consummate multi-tasker, so I may have erroneously referred to this as a lunch "date." Or maybe it was no accident.

Not that it wasn't romantic. Especially digging through our files to find copies of what we fondly refer to as "coffee money," aka our combined 401k accounts, Roth IRAs, and statements from some option we bought during one or another bubble.

Several years ago we sat down in a bright Dallas office of Charles Schwab and worked out a suitable asset allocation based on our low tolerance for risk and high desire to have a lot of money someday. After that, life interfered. The systematic review of our assets went the way of date nights. That is to say, it was neglected.

Then there was the whole stock market issue. Remember 2009? Or don't. Neither my husband nor I had the stomach to look at our accounts for months. I kept telling him, "Don't worry, everyone's in the same boat." When the communal sigh of relief was heard throughout the land as the Dow began to rise, our portfolio was still looking like a latte finance plan. I switched my encouragement to, "Don't be such a baby. It's not a trailer park; it's a mobile home community."

Because it was a date, and because my husband was coming from work, where he is still expected to wear something a notch up from yoga pants and flip flops, I dressed for our appointment with the banker. As I pulled on big girl slacks, I thought I'd better not gain weight, or lose it either. Ever. These may be the last nice clothes I'd ever own.

We were greeted, served coffee, and showed to an office where our retirement specialist explained to us the process of mapping out best case and acceptable case scenarios for our non-working future. We spent what I thought was an inordinate amount of time discussing the age at which my husband would retire.

"Fifty-five is ideal," he said.

"Are you kidding me?" I said. "That's in ten years. You have no hobbies. What would you do with the rest of your life?" And, I thought, I'll be fifty. My need for cosmetic procedures will just be ramping up and those are not cheap.

"Okay, sixty."

"Sixty-five."

"You know," the nice woman with the calculator said, "there are considerable benefits to waiting until you're sixty-seven to stop working."

"Ha!" I said. Such a romantic.

After a brief discussion of Social Security and far fewer questions about our saving and spending habits than I expected, we came to the "extras" section of the interview. This is where my husband asserted his need in retirement to buy a boat—a big one.

"Except I want to buy it now," he told our trusted counselor.

"Okay," she said. "We'll work that into the calculation." She turned to me. "One last question—how do you want me to treat your income? Should I count it as extra or include it in the overall forecast."

"Put it toward my world travels," I told her.

"Your travels?"

"Best case scenario."

She turned to John. "Did you know about the traveling?"

He shrugged. "She doesn't like my boat."

Top Ten Stupid Date Night Ideas

WITH THE RIDICULOUS DATE NIGHT ADVICE OUT THERE, IT'S A wonder anyone's having any fun at all. Here are the top ten stupid date night ideas I found on the Internet. (I swear I did not make these up.)

10. Put on your sexiest stilettos and sip fancy cocktails at a hotel bar.

I'm hoping the heels are for the ladies, but still. Watch your step. You won't feel too sexy on the stretcher en route to the nearest ER.

9. Bubble bath for two with candles and champagne.

Ah… the classic. Remember that what passes for sexy in the movies does not necessarily translate into your real life. Unless you really enjoy taking baths and you and your lovahhh can fit neatly into the tub together, this play might be out of your league. Then again, bubbles hide a multitude of [cheesecake] sins.

8. Make a meal of aphrodisiac oysters.

Slurping oysters from the shell is supposed to be hot. Perhaps, but if you're leery about tomatoes and bagged spinach, raw seafood may not be in your comfort zone.

7. Grown up trick-or-treating.

Again, I did not make this up. One site actually suggested putting on a sexy outfit and knocking on the bedroom door. This is disturbing and wrong. Plus, unless you're a size two, the naughty nurse costume is a little scary.

6. Enjoy a rousing game of Twister.

Uh huh. If you're going to try this, I suggest you first program the number of a great chiropractor into your cell phone and keep it within reach. Better yet, leave it with your neighbor, as she'll likely be the one to rescue you from your twisted little love knot.

5. Spread a blanket on the floor and have a carpet picnic.

Maybe your house is cleaner than mine. Maybe your carpet is newer. I'm just saying. Getting too close to my floor would quickly transform any romantic ideas into fantasies of having the steam cleaner guy come twice a year instead of once.

4. Take a sketchpad to a scenic bluff and draw your own version of the vista.

Is it just my husband, or would your guy also draw a stick figure with boobs?

3. Suit up and spend a late afternoon at the indoor pool of the YMCA.

Nothing gets me hotter than nasal burning chlorine and swimming in kid pee. You?

2. Paint coffee mugs at a paint-your-own-pottery place.

Seriously? Coffee mugs? Shoot me now.

And my all time favorite:

1. Give each other haircuts.

What can I say? I hope you have a pre-nup.

Marriage, Home Maintenance, and Imaginary Widowhood

IF HUSBANDS WERE LOTTERY PRIZES, MINE—WITH HIS FAT paycheck, full head of Richard Gere hair, and sly smile—would be the Power Ball. He takes care of his kids, makes me laugh, and is great in bed. (Don't tell him I said that—any of it.) Bonus: he's handy. Not snake-the-toilet handy—Bob Vila handy.

His skills have saved us thousands over the years, and currently subsidize my twice-monthly housekeeper habit. John changes oil and brakes, makes filtered water flow, and spackles my drywall. He doesn't complain about these jobs, which are always more difficult and time consuming than they should be.

He sighs and says, "Nothing's ever easy."

We fell in love with our house six years ago. Relocating from out of state, we had two harried realtors and forty-eight hours to make a decision. Our favorite feature was the two-story living room and its arched windows flooding light in every direction.

We didn't notice the six canister lights on the ceiling—twenty-five feet up—until some time after closing.

When we moved in I placed lamps all over the room and pretended the dull overhead lighting didn't exist. We could have lived like that forever without changing a single bulb if John hadn't insisted on using the damn things.

But you choose your battles. Especially when you live with the jackpot.

For years John pondered what to do at the first bulb fatality. When one of the easy-access lights in the kitchen popped, he replaced it at its ten-foot perch and sweated over the eventual death of one of those unreachable living room lights, trying to estimate how many hours of life remained. I humored him, joining debates over the relative merits of ladders versus scaffolding versus accessing the cans through the attic. It always ended with John imploring the cosmos, "Why the hell would anyone put lights up so high?"

It was immoral.

When the inevitable happened it hit him hard. John spent weeks looking at the ceiling, searching for his strategy. I discovered he'd opted for the attic route when I was folding laundry and a light casing crashed to the floor, accompanied by a grunt. He'd have to fix that now too.

But damn it, he'd changed the bulb!

He beamed coming down the stairs. The glow disappeared when he flipped the switch to find it still dead. He'd missed the location and replaced one perfectly good bulb with another. I reminded him that we didn't need to turn on those lights. Ever. But he insisted, so we agreed to change them all at once. I suggested hiring a service. Once you pay someone to clean the toothpaste ring out of your bathroom sink, there's not much you won't outsource.

John wanted to do the job himself so we moved furniture and rugs, and leaned a borrowed ladder against the wall. Wanting to be as useful as my prize of a husband, I planned to do a thorough cleaning under the sofas where I expected to find entire colonies of dust loving creatures. All I found was the shiny wood flooring John installed last winter.

Clearly, the cleaning lady needed a raise.

As my devoted husband climbed, the ladder wobbled terribly. How could I not picture him plummeting to the floor like two hundred ten pounds of raw meat? I wondered what widowhood might look like. Adrenaline shot through my core as I realized I'd probably have to give up the housekeeper.

I noticed the weight limit on the shaky aluminum ladder: two hundred pounds. "Careful, Babe."

We moved around the room, him taking new and old bulbs on each trip up and down the shaky ladder and me with my foot firmly wedged at its base. I knew that should something go wrong, my hundred and twenty pounds wouldn't stop any tragedy and could in fact, render my children orphans. (Oh sure they'd love it, but that's another essay). Once we had a system going, my mind wandered.

What would I do if he fell? It's not like I could score another like him. Hitting the Power Ball is a once in a lifetime deal. Once you've won, what's the point of wasting your money on scratch-off tickets? Still, I made a mental note to Google "respectable period of mourning." I do look great in black.

Concentrating to keep my post at the ladder, my eyes were on John's legs, but my mind escaped to that great looking guy in the carpool line and the green-eyed boy at The Gap who almost sold me those awful jeans because he kept saying my name. This imaginary widowhood was nothing but a harmless fantasy, right?

I wondered where John had been while they were selling tickets to the awesome wife lottery.

Of course I was relieved—happy even—when he came down safely from the ladder that final time. Jackpot husband intact. Only a fool would dream of anything else. But in case I decide to further indulge the dark side of my imagination, I'll have my chance.

Tomorrow he's checking bent roof tiles.

The Journey

Are We There Yet?

THIS YEAR I BOUGHT AIRLINE TICKETS FOR AUGUST IN APRIL. That's how far in advance I planned our summer vacation. Not exactly spontaneous. As I confirmed the reservations, I wondered when summer vacation morphed from something that exemplified pure freedom to just another obligation. When had it become a mere set of squares on the calendar to coordinate?

When we were kids, the last day of school and the first day of the next school year may as well have been decades apart. All we knew was trips and reading lists and sleeping in. We had water-slides, watermelon, and trout fishing. And the end was too far away to imagine. Just like those long car trips where we could not help ourselves but ask, "Are we there yet?"

By the time we hit the more permissive middle school years, we had traded jumpers for bikinis. Summer meant drinking ulcer-inducing quantities of Diet Coke, watching MTV until our eyes bled, and taking sex quizzes in Cosmo—all while baking in the sun under a healthy coating of baby oil mixed with iodine. We were all pink cheeks and blonde streaks, earned honestly at the seaside or pool. In high school we had summer jobs and summer loves. We sneaked out and drank wine coolers until dawn. The college years brought more of the same, only legal this time. Those became the summers against which all future Junes, Julys, and Augusts would be judged. If ever we were there, that was the time. And we thought it would last forever.

But it didn't last long. We grew up and went to work and packed up summer vacation with our varsity jackets and mix tapes. Highlights were acquired at the salon, and the rosy pink glow came courtesy of Cover Girl. The closest we came to liberty was sneaking out of the office early to hit Happy Hour, and maybe a week off for good behavior. The sun still brought fun, but even when business was slow, there wasn't much difference between summer and the rest of the year. Days were spent in cubicles wishing we were anywhere but there.

Then we had kids and their summer schedule dominated ours. Simply taking care of them during non-school hours became a challenge. Working parents scrambled for childcare and their stay-at-home counterparts scraped at their own fragile sanity in a house overrun by children. There was tennis practice and drama camp, the junior botany club, and something down at the library with Elmer's glue and sequins. Summer seemed more like a prison sentence than a get-out-of-jail-free card. Even the pool was a chore. We knew that SPF 50 was probably overkill, but a kid's sunburn might get us hauled into Child Services. Weeks zipped by on the calendar faster than we could pencil in a day at the lake and a trip to grandma's house.

It was our children's turn to ask, "Are we there yet?"

Soon they will have their own jobs, and cars that carry them away for frighteningly long stretches of time. If you're like me, you can't help but wonder what you'll do when your little birds fly the nest.

I can tell you exactly what you'll be doing.

Working.

Someone's got to pay for all that fun. And you wouldn't have it any other way, would you? It's the natural evolution of summer. The result, however, is that the next time you can expect to have anything resembling the carefree joy of your youthful summers will be sometime after 2030.

Meet me at Happy Hour and we'll gum some corn chips and suck down a virgin margarita.

Are we there yet?

Not in the *Frommer's Guide to New York City*

LAST SUMMER WE TOOK OUR FIRST TRIP TO NEW YORK. I FAITH-fully studied the *Frommer's Guide to New York City With Kids* to find the perfect place to park our suburban family for the two-day trip. The financial district turned out to be surprisingly low-key and family friendly over the weekend. Despite our tourist status, it didn't take long to feel like New Yorkers.

I even figured out the subway. The first day we found our way onto the red line, headed to the Museum of Natural History. Smug, I watched another family openly consulting the Frommer's Guide I'd wisely tucked into my backpack. Rookies.

We bounced along until my son inexplicably hopped up and walked off the train at Canal Street—a full 673 blocks early. He had one foot on the platform before I sprung from my seat and pulled him back in. Crisis averted.

"I could totally live here," I said, more to myself than anyone else. My husband rolled his eyes.

I held onto my son until we safely reached the museum, where, following my carefully crafted itinerary, we saw as many of the most important exhibits as possible. (Including an unplanned sighting of Carolina Herrera, next to a panorama of Great Plains—and yes, her white shirt is crisper than yours.) When it was time for lunch we found the perfect pizza place exactly where the book had promised.

"I could totally live here," I said later, watching my kids play air guitar on a rock in Central Park.

"You think?" My husband wasn't convinced.

That next day we took a tour of the harbor and ate overpriced pasta on Pier 16. Afterwards we walked along the waterfront of Battery Park City, an area full of Frisbees, dogs, and strollers. The guidebook had highlighted the playground just two blocks from our hotel as a key perk of the location. Once again, Frommer's didn't disappoint.

Our children swung in the tires, climbed the rope net, and slid down the fireman's pole with real city kids while my husband and I found a bench to relax and keep an eye on them. With the sun setting, and the slightest chill in the air—just enough to bring us closer together on the bench—we felt completely at home. Like a couple of locals.

"I could totally live here," I told my husband again.

"Nah." He reminded me that everything we owned in suburbia—the house, the cars, the boat, the stainless steel refrigerator—would buy us approximately six hundred square feet in New York City.

As we enjoyed our last night in the city, vowing to come back soon, three very cool teenaged girls—the kind you might see on one of those reality shows I'm too old to know the name of— approached the playground equipment. The tallest, longest-haired, hottest-bodied of the three immediately grasped the pole directly in front of us and began demonstrating to her friends how to work it. Twirling, sliding, grinding. Clearly, she had practice. My husband squirmed, simultaneously watching and averting his eyes. I searched my pockets for ones.

"Well…" I said. "That wasn't in the guidebook."

The closest thing we have to this kind of entertainment at home is when an Arbor Mist loving girlfriend hosts one of those parties where you're supposed to buy your own personal stripper pole and install it in your bedroom. (Because your children would certainly never ask, hey mom, why are you hanging off that pole?) A friend of mine recently had one built into her new house from the upstairs down into the laundry room. She calls it a fireman's pole, swears it's for the kids to slide down. Right, that's why the laundry room also has a chaise lounge and a deadbolt.

The free show continued for some time as the beta girls took turns emulating their erotic alpha. It didn't bother me, so long as my daughter was oblivious. And when my husband recovered from his initial shock, he turned to me and said,

"I could totally live here."

Camping, Anyone?

It was the hottest day of the year. Naturally, we decided to camp. But first, for added amusement, we spent the entire ninety-plus degree day on the lake with friends. All day we soaked in the sun and its glare off the water. Grownups quenched thirst with beer while kids gorged on Cheetos and orange soda. We all got sunburned. As the hour got later and hotter, friends questioned our choice to sleep in a tent. But we truly believed it would be fun.

Around six, when everyone else docked their boats and headed for the air-conditioned Nirvana of their suburban homes, we trailered up and parked ourselves at the campsite. A friend waved goodbye, saying "I'll be thinking of you tonight, when I flip my pillow over to the cool side."

But we knew. We KNEW how to have fun. Not like those wimpy homebodies. We had hotdogs and 'tater salad and all the makings for perfect s'mores. First, we built a fire. My husband thinks of everything. Never mind it was ninety-five degrees without a breeze. How else would we cook the hotdogs? While the fire blazed, the kids complained. Even the lake—by now one huge bathtub—offered no comfort. I gave my children ice from the cooler, which they rubbed on their reddened skin. The dog hung his head.

"It'll be fine once the sun goes down," my husband reassured.

But he was wrong. Somehow the temperature increased after sundown. Even melted chocolate and marshmallow could not lift our spirits. In the darkness, we sat—around the place where the obligatory campfire had been. When it got too hot to expend the energy necessary to make up stories, we went to bed. And by bed, I mean the ground, cushioned by a generous layer of nylon tent floor. Our spacious four-man (yeah, right) tent offered the added benefit of trapping the now liquid air.

The children and I whined and feverishly fanned ourselves with paper plates. Finally, we pleaded with my husband to go home. He wouldn't hear of it.

"It wouldn't be so hot if you quit complaining, you pansies."

Our protests affect the air temperature, apparently. But you know what they say: pick your battles. So I sucked it up and persuaded the kids to do the same. We suffered in silence until I felt I might actually suffocate. I sat up and pressed my face next to the tent "window," hoping to get some oxygen through the nylon mesh.

"What are you doing?" my husband asked.

"Oh, nothing, Babe. Just breathing."

That's all it took—fear of spousal asphyxiation—to convince my husband it was time to go. The kids leaped into action. In the dark we packed the boat in record time. Our quickness was fueled by the joyful anticipation of sweet, cool A/C. I swear the dog smiled.

Five minutes out of the campsite the air temperature dropped ten degrees. But that was nothing compared to the icy cotton at home, on the flipside of my pillow.

Could Be Worse

Bloody, brutal, bone-chilling Squirt level hockey. That's
what compelled us to drive five hours in the snow. We'd made
good time to St. Louis, without so much as a missed exit, and
checked into a Holiday Inn just off I-55. I took credit for that. A
check of the coach's email confirmed we only had time for a
quick pee before heading to the ice rink so the nine- and
eleven-year olds could skate to certain victory—or at least a
consolation medal. With fifty pounds of reeking hockey gear,
we headed to our first game.

*Note: Good hockey moms Febreeze (yes, that's a verb) and/or launder
hockey clothes and equipment weekly. I prefer a good scrubbing
annually. Call me green.*

We piled into the Dorito-littered car, mapped the route on my
handy i-can-quit-anytime phone, and headed north on I-55.

"What did we do before we had GPS?" my husband asked.

"We called people on the phone and they said things like, take the 54th Street exit and turn right on Maple."

No need for unreliable human contact now. I had a Super Phone.

"It could be worse," I told my family when my husband took the wrong ramp—the one that led to the graffiti district in downtown St. Louis. "It could be dark." No one appreciated my joke.

After a quick tour of rundown factories with barred, broken windows, colorful wisdom sprayed onto the walls, and too many one-way streets, we found the highway that led to the Illinois suburb hosting the hockey tournament. (Yes, our game was in a different state than our hotel.) We had barely lost five minutes; my baby girl, the star defenseman, and my son, super wingman, would make it to the game on time.

Though my husband wasn't saying so, I know he thought the wrong turn was my fault, and maybe it was. Sure, I was navigating, but he was the one turning the steering wheel. At least the phone battery was charged and the little blinking ball that represented our car on the map was back on track. It could have been worse.

"Are you sure this is the way?" my children asked six hundred and forty-seven times.

"Of course I am." I held up screen with the digital image of the map. "See."

Twenty minutes later we were lost again. This time it really was my fault, or rather my phone's fault. The GPS missed a turnoff that led to Fairview Heights. We were headed to Chicago. I called the rink for directions to I-64 and our exit just before the coach called in a panic over the absence of his two star players.

"We're almost there," I told him. "Exit twelve, right? Off sixty-four?"

"Uh—I came in on fifty-five, so... not sure."

"Okay, well, we'll be there A-S-A-P."

We were at the exit in minutes, within a mile of the rink. And with ten minutes to spare. We would have made it with no problem, if some genius hadn't put the hockey rink too close to the shopping mall. In the crawling Saturday afternoon traffic, my husband's face grew tighter and grayer at the eternity of each stoplight. He changed into the right lane, only to have the left move faster.

To diffuse the stressful situation I screamed toward the back-seat, "Stop talking!"

"We didn't say anything."

"Whatever," I said. "Quit complaining. It could be worse."

In the ensuing quiet, my synapses fired. I-55, really? Coach got here on I-55? Because according to my virtual map we were nowhere near I-55.

"That would be funny," I said, thinking out loud, "if we were going to the wrong rink." The crease in between my husband's brows grew deeper. The kids groaned. I double-checked the email with the rink address and reassured everyone, "We're totally going to the right place."

We found the street the rink was on. It was a dead end. However, we could see the building through the trees just yards away. My husband looked at me and raised his eyebrows.

"I'm going for it."

He jumped the curb, burned around a couple of trees, and bounced into the parking lot like a triumphant Clark Griswold pulling up to Wallyworld. I told him to pull up in front, unload, and I'd park the car. Just as my family had taken out the last of the hockey bags, the coach called again.

"How close are you?"

"We're here," I told him. I looked at red letters on the side of the rink. "US Hockey, right?"

Horrible silence filled the line.

"Uh—no. We're at American Hockey."

Of course they were.

"Didn't you get my email last night?"

"No, Coach, I didn't get your email." Behind the car, frustration turned to anger. Gear thudded back into the car, doors were slammed, and the look on my husband's face was—not good.

With the smelly bags and players reloaded, I hit the reverse route button on the mapping app and we headed back, rolling south on I-55 through downtown St. Louis, back the way we had come, with the Gateway Arch as a backdrop. This time it was getting dark; this time we didn't get lost. I called the coach and told him we'd try and make the second half.

"Get dressed," my husband told the kids. "We didn't come all this way to miss these games!" They wiggled into their gear in the back seat.

My husband was not finding the humor, so I tried not to laugh. Tension in the car was high, but it shouldn't have been. Who wants to watch four hockey games in one weekend anyway? So we were late to one game? It's not a real problem, not like washing your favorite jeans with your best lip plumper in the pocket, or having to drive the Lexus when your Mercedes is in the shop.

To be a hockey family is to be privileged. The rink fees, the gear, the camps—it's not cheap. And to travel on top of it? We spend a fortune going to other cities with their hotel rooms and over-priced breakfast buffets only to watch our kids get pummeled by host teams who only organize tournaments to subsidize their huge winning trophies. And it's always the home team that wins. So what if we missed a game? It could be worse.

One of the other dads called to tell me we were up by two, as if, after getting lost three times and spending nearly an hour on the road, we cared about the score. We cared less even when we found out that the right rink was not only not in another state, but actually only five minutes from our hotel.

"Love to be a fly on that windshield," someone joked when we arrived "It's like that movie, right? Vacation or something?"

Exactly, except that in our car, unlike the movies, there are no punch lines—only clipped responses and deep cleansing breaths.

"At least we got to see the Arch," my husband said. "Twice."

On the ice, my son scrambled back from the box because he forgot his gloves. My daughter scored an assist in her first two-minute shift. I got to yell at a corrupt referee, "Does that whistle even work?" And that night our kids played harder at 'wrestle hockey' next to the pool at the hotel than they did on the ice. It was no surprise we didn't win the championship. But we did come in second. And for that we got—

"Just…" my husband said with a sigh, "…ribbons."

But it's not about winning. We do it to create memories our children will carry into adulthood. Good memories, we hope. Maybe a happy childhood will cushion some of the pain of adulthood. I suspect though, that the memories they keep will have little to do with the thrill of a goal or the rush of a win, and more to do with those moments of screaming in the car. I just hope that in retrospect, like in the movies, they make them laugh. Because it could be worse. Our troubles could have nothing to do with botched directions and frustrated parental venting. I hope my children someday know that, and realize just how good they had it.

I also hope they remember their dad's screaming more vividly than they remember mine.

Meet Me at the Hotel Room

REMEMBER WHEN HOTEL ROOMS WERE SEXY? ALL VACATION AND rendezvous and sheets you didn't have to clean? Me neither. But I do remember when a hotel room represented relaxation, time away from the responsibilities of regular life, family life. Hotels were all about freshly made beds, hours of freedom, drinks mixed with ice from down the hall. And again, the lack of laundry.

Now I have children so most of my disposable income goes toward giving them all those advantages I never had. These experiences are supposed serve them later in life, or create wonderful memories—maybe even emotional security. Who knows? All I know right now is: travel sports.

In between games, hotel rooms have become an agony of too much family togetherness. Where once there was vacation, now there is obligation. Where once there was soft lighting and exotic snacks, now there are wet towels and fights over burgers versus Mexican. Where once there were cute little bottles of conditioner I didn't need, now there are my tweens' ever expanding collections of grooming aids, which are fast outgrowing my own. The hotel bed seems small when shared with my daughter—the one who will be as tall as I am in one quick inch.

Instead of a good movie on TV (possibly featuring a half-naked Mark Wahlberg), we are forced to suffer through endless half-hours of Miley Cyrus and that guy with the mullet whose achy breaky heart we all wanted to crush—with a sledgehammer—back in 1992. And the beds, which are quickly unmade to rid them of the microbe-infested bedspreads, are covered with soggy pizza boxes. (Okay, maybe that part's the same.)

In a hotel room with my family, I hide in the bathroom reading a book, partly to be alone, and partly so that no one can stink up the 200 square feet that have become our communal living space.

Did I mention the dog? Oh yes, we are that family. And because we don't want to spend any more than necessary, we do not pay the hotel's pet fee, but instead choose to smuggle the dog in and out of the room, begging him to "go" at our convenience.

In close proximity to the ever present them, I grow increasingly irritated. I crave escape from my husband's brilliant observations, such as "This place really fills up at night" and the kids' constant need for food and distraction. When the bathroom fails to provide refuge, I turn to the ill-equipped fitness center where I am devastated to see that although there are only two lonely treadmills, the tiny room has been outfitted with three walls of floor to ceiling mirrors, allowing me to see all that is shielded in my own strategically mirrored home. I want to go there. Home. Now.

Other parents have already crossed back into the world of peaceful hotel rooms. They have begun to reserve two rooms; one for themselves and one for the kids. I can't do that. I'm cheap, remember? Besides, I'd miss my daughter kicking me in the face on that tiny, pizza-scented bed.

Great Racing Dragons

I RECENTLY CAME ACROSS A SECTION OF NEWSPAPER I'D BEEN saving. On the front page of Local Section, Wednesday, December 29th, 2004, is my son, riding his bike—in a purple dragon costume. His chin is tilted up, maybe because he's trying to see the road through the white, felt dragon teeth that cover his face. Big lavender dragon eyes perch atop his head. Horns stick out and black "smoke" comes out of the creature's nostrils. I see the gap where a 6-year-old tooth used to be, and the dragon snout is like the bill of a cap on my little boy's head.

Why is my kid on a bike in a dragon suit? And how did this moment happen to be captured in newsprint? Blame his parents. My husband and I have no shame. Also, we were bored.

During one of the long, cold days of winter break, while we were minding our own business looking out the window, we saw a newspaper photographer taking pictures of some neighbor boys racing down the hill on their new motorized scooters. We didn't like those boys. They're the same ones who shoot bottle rockets at us every Fourth of July. Plus, our son is way cuter.

Those other kids didn't deserve to be in the paper, but ours did. Problem was he didn't get a fancy new toy for Christmas—mostly because of the mortgage payment. While he happily built Lego Bionicles and made up their pretend lives, we pondered our dilemma: How to get our son in the paper?

Letting him drive the car around the block was out of the question, of course. But think, think…

Halloween! Now there's a holiday. Despite my frugal tendencies, that year I had caved to heart wrenching pleas in the seasonal aisle. Thanks to our friendly Walmart costume buyer and lots of child labor Somewhere Else, my children had worn fabulous and warm Lion-King-worthy costumes. (The Broadway version, not that thing your kids put on in the school cafeteria.) We summoned our son from his non-attention-getting fun.

"Do you still have that Dragon costume?"

"Why?"

"Put it on and go ride your bike." Snicker, snicker. His face registered confusion, but we feed him so he has to do what we say.

Five minutes later my boy was riding up and down the street, dragon head bobbing up and down in shameless self-promotion. The reporter soon abandoned the older boys and took shot after shot of our pride and joy as we convulsed with laughter from our vantage point. Seriously, I almost peed.

It's not like he didn't enjoy wearing the dragon costume. He and his sister had played with those things a dozen times since Halloween. The fact that he'd never thought to leave the house in it just proves how much he's got to learn. And we, as his parents, are charged with the duty to teach, are we not?

The reporter was giggling when she knocked on the door to get his name. The newspaper titled the picture "Dragon Racer." But that's not important. What is: those other boys didn't end up in the paper—and mine did.

Best Mom Ever: Ski Instructor

WE'VE ALL SEEN THAT PSYCHO MOM BARKING ORDERS AT HER KIDS like a drill sergeant after one too many lattes. You want to pass her a Valium and rescue the kids from a lifetime of therapy. You know her?

She's me.

As soon as my husband uttered the words, "ski vacation," I was all over it. Within minutes I had visited the resort's website and whipped out a spreadsheet complete with activities, restaurants, and a budget. I printed Mapquest directions and loaded up on Nintendo DS games for the drive. I rocked the planning phase. Still, as our departure date approached, I hadn't yet made ski school reservations.

"Did you call?" my husband asked for the hundredth time on the twelve-hour drive to the mountain.

"It'll be fine." Did he appreciate all I'd done? Why did he have to harp on those damn ski school reservations?

At the resort, I lost myself in awe of the perfect symmetry of a single snowflake on my gloves, finding comfort in that six-spoked creation. The snowflake doesn't disappoint; it's always picture-book-perfect, just like our ski vacation.

Imagine my surprise the next morning, after hiking up sixteen flights of stairs in Gortex and boots to find that ski school was full. Oops. We promptly signed the kids up for the next day and decided to salvage the day by skiing with them. On the walk to the rental shop I chastised myself for wrecking the day while my husband pretended not to be irked. We suffered through long lines, our children's professional grade whining, and too-tight boots before heading to our doom on the slopes.

After twenty minutes of "I can't!" and, "It doesn't work," along with some hateful silence, I'd had enough. I couldn't take another namby pamby minute. Suddenly single-minded in purpose, I declared that we were leaving the bunny slope. Twenty minutes later I was screaming down the first run.

Dig in!

Pay attention!

Toes together!

Get up! Get UP! GET UP!!!

Sure, I looked insane and I scared a few kids who weren't mine. Whatever. It's not like I don't know better. I know how I should have been acting. I should have been sensitive to my children's feelings, protected their precious sense of accomplishment, and coddled their fragile self-esteem.

That's just not me.

Maybe I felt a little bad being so tough on my kids. Maybe there were a few tears inside their goggles, and yes, other parents judged me. What can I say? I'm no snowflake. If I'd let all that stuff deter me, my kids would have missed a whole day of skiing.

Instead, within an hour my shouts had changed from maniacal to:

Good!

You got it!

Now you're skiing!

SHRED!!!

Any residue of guilt fell away that night when I tucked my kids into the soft hotel sheets.

"Mom," my daughter said, wrapping warm fingers around my neck. "You're the Best Mom Ever."

"No," I said, kissing her on the cheek.

"Uh-huh," my son added.

"You think?"

They nodded.

"Best Mom Ever!" we all screamed.

A few days later I watched another couple try to smooth talk their son off the ground.

"See all the other kids?" Mama cooed. "You can do it!"

"Come on, Conner," Daddy pleaded.

"Pleeeeze," they both practically cried.

The kid just sat there, holding all the power.

If the soft approach works for you, go for it, but know that you can't fake sensitive. Kids smell artifice like a dog senses fear. Better to be yourself, even though you're not perfect. Quit trying to be a snowflake. It's SO much better to be the Best Mom Ever!

Until Further Notice

"Don't you think we should turn back?" I asked my husband when the snow surrounded us completely.

"No."

"What if that happens again?"

"I'll slow down," he said. Excellent. We'd plummet *slowly* to our deaths.

Just over the pass, ten-foot amber lights announced: Highway 87 Closed Until Further Notice.

Looking around at the cars ahead of and behind us, I knew we needed a room, and quick. "Get the one with the pool," I said, pointing to the Comfort Inn.

The next day I watched horizontal snow while one after another all roads heading out of New Mexico were systematically closed.

LELA DAVIDSON

"They've set up a shelter at the high school gymnasium," my husband said. We'd been among the last lucky travelers to get a hotel room, and thus avoid the National Guard cots and Red Cross soup.

Instead, we had fast food and a debit card. In a crisis, it's important to have a plan. That day ours was to stuff ourselves on lunch at McDonald's so we wouldn't have to brave the icy evening. We ordered several super-sized meals, inhaled them, and bought more.

"Here, finish this off," my husband said, shoving a mostly eaten cheeseburger at me. I grunted. Then I ate it. You can't be too careful. Besides, the nutritional value of food eaten under duress doesn't count. No calories, no carbs, no fat grams. Remember that next time you are snowbound in the vicinity of a Big Mac. Or two.

The food situation scared me. Although I had hoarded my share of oatmeal packets and cherry Danishes from the hotel's continental breakfast, I couldn't help thinking with all those people stuck in one place we could run out of food. "We need emergency supplies," I announced.

Into the SUV we piled, off to the grocery store for peanut butter and jelly, bread, and Oreos. I also grabbed a tabloid because that's another vice that doesn't count in a blizzard. My rule.

That night I surfed the web, read, and checked email while the kids bickered in the background. My husband watched man TV. Just like home. Except at home I had laundry and cooking. This extended vacation offered maids and Nintendo DS to babysit the kids. Until further notice.

I became an expert at tracking expected snowfall and wind speed, at finding highways on maps. I knew the wind that whipped off the mesa on Highway 87 caused fifteen-foot snow-drifts, which had claimed one of the two snowplows in the area. I knew Vegas, Raton Pass, and Springer like a local. (It only took a couple of days to realized it wasn't *that* Vegas.) Still, by the third day in Shangri-La, my husband and I began to question what would happen in the event of a true emergency. Would we hear that alarming BEEEEP from the radio and TV directing us where to go and what to do? Because this felt like rather a good time for some direction. No one seemed to be in charge.

~⚬~

The next morning we woke to open roads and hit them. Flat, snow-covered land never looked so good. Sunshine and ice-covered grasses turned the sparse landscape into a diamond-encrusted dream. But just short of the promised land of Texas, the road closed again.

"It's ten miles to the state line," I said. "Go for it!" When my husband gunned it around the roadblock that held us hostage, ten cars followed. Just over the Texas line, the snow began to grow around us and I felt my gut tighten. We saw the backside of another roadblock. Thankfully, the officer on duty looked the other way while we drove past it through a space just wide enough for one car.

Ahead lay bare pavement and the Texas plains. I wanted to hang out the window and lift my top in victory. I settled instead for a whoop-whoop fist pump out the passenger side window. Then I put all future travel plans on hold—until further notice.

Me Time

Anti-Resolutions

SELF-IMPROVEMENT IS OVERRATED. THIS YEAR INSTEAD OF vowing to be better and then letting myself down two weeks later, I'm taking a different approach. I'm making anti-resolutions. That way if I succeed I'm successful, and if I fail I'm successful too.

I resolve to gain weight.

This should be a fun one. Who wants to be skinny anyway? Just think of all the new shopping I'll get to do when I can no longer zip my jeans—to say nothing of the joy of Brie and chocolate. And once I gain all that weight, I'm going to start a foundation similar to Locks of Love, except instead of donating hair to cancer patients, we'll get lipo-sucked and donate the results to runway models.

I resolve to stop working out.

It might be difficult to find the time to not exercise, but a little determination goes a long way. Marathons of the Real House-wives on Bravo will help. And hello—double bonus, no workout clothes means less laundry! Who needs extra energy and long life?

I resolve to start smoking.

So many people smoke, I'm starting to wonder what I'm missing. Seriously, if it's so hard to quit it must be pretty good, right? However, I've heard smoking helps keep the weight off so this could make my resolution to gain weight more difficult. I'm willing to take the chance. Besides, considering the state of my retirement account, a shorter life expectancy makes sense.

I resolve to increase my alcohol intake.

Next year at my annual physical I'd like to move my answer from the 3-5 drinks per week to the 5-8 category. It's a realistic goal. Combined with the weight gain, lack of exercise, and smoking, this resolution has the potential to make a real impression on my overall health—and my physician.

I resolve to mess up the garage.

I've been trying to organize our garage for five years. (By organize I mean I've been trying to get my husband to pick up his stuff and get rid of the junk he calls "tools".) At this point I'm ready to give it up to the family of squirrels that have taken to eating the dog food the children drop on the floor.

I resolve to spend less quality time with the family.

Do you ever get the feeling your family takes you for granted? I do, and I think a little extended absence from Mama is what they need to make their hearts grow fonder. I'm thinking of a solo tour of Europe.

I resolve to decrease my charitable contributions.

Aren't I helping the world enough by spending money on my $4 cups of coffee and my 38 pairs of black shoes? All those unfortunate people don't need the money like I do—Retrinol doesn't grow on trees, you know.

I resolve to decrease my vocabulary.

Some of the words floating around my brain have very little purpose in my everyday life and frankly I need to free up some capacity to stay on top of Facebook updates. Autumn for example—who needs it? Fall is shorter and more descriptive. Autumn, you're dead to me.

I resolve to make less money.

This one needs some clarification. Let's be clear that I don't want to have less money or spend less money, I just don't want to be the person who earns it.

When You Want to Run Away

WHEN I WAS A KID I NEVER FANTASIZED ABOUT RUNNING AWAY TO join the circus. Now that I'm older, I get it. Although it's not my dream to tame lions or become the bearded lady, I understand the lure of escaping to some exotic life where the tightrope you walk is literal as opposed to the figurative balancing act we do here in the world of diapers, homework, and ear infections.

My mother tells a story about her mother, who would tell her children that if they didn't behave she would run off to Tucumcari, New Mexico and they'd never find her. To which my mother responded that they most certainly would find her—in Tucumcari, New Mexico.

Mom shouted similar warnings to my brother and I as kids. She would run away and never return. We didn't have reason to believe her empty threats, but then again, you never knew. Moms are crazy like that. Our mothers and grandmothers didn't mess with balance—work, life, or otherwise. They didn't have spa days or antidepressants or Oprah. They just woke up in the morning and did what needed doing. And if they lost it once in a while, well, they were entitled.

Genetics notwithstanding, I have yet to issue such a circus-running-off sort of threat. I find that short periods of actual escape ward off visions of long-term flight. Running off for weekend writing classes and conferences recharges my depleted mama batteries and gives me strength to face the days of infinite laundry and incessant requests for double A batteries. I schedule my respites months in advanced and write them on the calendar in pen. In Sharpie.

My retreats may not be as exciting as swallowing swords, but for me, some quality time with a spiral notebook and a half decent pen is usually enough to return myself to equilibrium. And if it's not, I run off to yoga class, where we make like a tree and stand on one leg, or rest our thighs upon our biceps. That's balance. These are the things that keep me from losing it.

So next time you're tempted to run away, remember that you can juggle fire in the kitchen and rig up a tightrope in your own backyard. Just make sure you wait until after you've finished all that other balancing—you know, the checkbook, the food groups, and the quality time spent with each child.

And if you hear of any writers' meetings in Tucumcari, New Mexico, don't come looking for me.

Thank God I'm a Country Girl

THE FIRST THING I NOTICED WAS THE TRAILER ON THE FRONT lawn. The few times I'd met Sherri her mother had been with her, so I thought that must be where she lives. What a sweet woman, that Sherri, keeping Mama on the front lawn.

Next, I saw the enormous turkey, a hurkin' free-range bird who'd spend a season feasting on apples before Thanksgiving dinner. Look at me in the country, identifying barnyard creatures! I'd come a long way since my first day in Arkansas.

"What are those?" I had asked my husband on the drive in.

"What are what?"

"Those miniature cow-looking things," I said, pointing out the window.

"The goats?"

Thank God I'm a country girl.

Inside the house I was eager to show off my countrification. I asked Sherri's husband, Larry, all about the turkey.

"That's not a turkey," he assured me. Although I was pretty confident it was indeed a turkey, I'm too smart to argue with a man who owns a framed photo of George W and keeps a gun cabinet in the living room.

"Looks like a bobcat," said Sherri's mother.

Larry got the binoculars. "I think that's a skunk," he said.

"Could be a bobcat," Mother said.

"That's a skunk, all right." Larry was sure now.

"Or a bobcat," Mother said.

By this time other guests had arrived and the turkey/bobcat/skunk had hidden behind a tree. Larry disappeared too, as men do when a room fills with estrogen. We ladies got to chatting and forgot all about the beast until a screech filled the room.

"Skunk!" Sherri's sister-in-law shouted, having missed out on the earlier debate.

My previous experience with skunks consisted of Pepe Le Pew cartoons. This animal was neither charming nor French.

Apparently it wasn't even acting like a skunk, which I learned is a nocturnal animal. (Country girl, yes?) He shouldn't have been out before dark and he certainly had no business waddling around the way he was, like a bum high on Mad Dog. Turns out there's nothing like a rabid skunk to liven up a party. Sherri's sister-in-law gushed at the prospect of shooting something and promptly called the men. Larry appeared in the yard almost instantly with a rifle and a friend. Before I knew it, snap-pop-dead-skunk.

Kind of handy, that gun cabinet.

Deeply steeped in the ways of the country, we continued our party, barely noticing the odor of deceased, diseased rodent. When things started to wrap up, Larry appeared again in the kitchen. He filled his plate with tacos and fixin's from the Mexican hat lazy Susan, then walked out the front door.

"Where's he going?" I asked.

"Back out to his trailer," Sherri said.

Aha! It wasn't a mom trailer at all. It was a Man Trailer! That explained why he had come so quickly to remedy the wild animal situation. Good for Larry. He had his own personal territory where females would not tread. And he wasn't the only one. Other women told of tool sheds, campers, and detached garages. Why hadn't I thought of that?

After I'd said my goodbyes, I rolled slowly down the long gravel driveway. Blue light emanated from the Man Trailer and I

wondered at this curious habitat. What did it hold? Dirty magazines? Band saws? Beer? I'd never know, but I left the party
feeling humbled by the country, awed by its untamed creatures,
and impressed with the unexpected merits of keeping a trailer
on the front lawn.

How Do You Take Your Boo?

By NOW YOU MUST BE FAMILIAR WITH THE SUBURBAN RITUAL OF "Booing" one's neighbor with a basket of Halloween delights. Depending on my mood—and yes, there are many—I either love or hate the Boo.

The first time it happened I welcomed the cheerful ghost at my door, eagerly read the directions, shopped for goodies, and under cover of darkness delivered a treat bucket to my favorite neighbor. Since then, the Boo has gotten complicated.

First, you can't Boo just anyone. You have to choose someone who will keep the Boo going. (And who are we kidding here, it's Mom's job.) If you leave your secret treat on the door of a Boo Killer, the fun stops. And whose fault is that? Sure, she killed the Boo, but aren't you also to blame for your careless Boo selection? Phone calls are made. Accusations fly. Meanwhile, no further Booing occurs. To avoid this nasty situation, you carefully consult the neighborhood directory prior to initiating the Boo, considering the age and interests of the children, the family's overall propensity to be festive, and any current obligations that may hinder Boo participation.

Once you choose the right family to Boo—the one you know in your jack-o-lantern of a heart will honor the tradition—you must find items for the basket that will produce the intended result: excitement for Halloween, and by extension, the entire holiday season. Screw up the Boo and there won't be a decent potluck until Easter. So you go to the store for a pumpkin pacifier and a bag of orange rawhides for your neighbor who has a baby and two Rottweilers. Minutes before you're set to Boo and run, you notice they've already been Boo'd! Yes, you've been beaten to the Boo. Now you have to start all over with the choosing and the shopping and the sneaking around the bushes. Sometimes, you even have to Boo someone you don't even like. It's enough to make Christmas look easy.

Occasionally all goes as planned. You choose the correct Boo recipient and appropriate candies and novelties, but wait—are they good enough? Because of course the Boo is competitive. This is suburbia, silly. No one wants to give a "bad" Boo basket, so the goodies get increasingly more extravagant each year. (Though I've yet to receive a bottle of Tanqueray.) No matter how carefully you choose your lucky Boo receiver or how thoughtfully you shop, someone will always have a better Boo than you.

For the past couple of years I've considered quietly bowing out of the Booing altogether. I know women who place a pre-emptive Boo sign on the door, fraudulently indicating that they've already been Boo'd, already completed their end of this ghoulish social contract. Sneaky and effective; I like it. But I also love the fun and community of the Boo.

That's why I believe the time has come for a Boo Gift Registry. We can streamline this process. Admit it, between the Halloween lights, the Hobby Lobby scarecrow, and all those classroom parties, none of us has time to navigate the subtleties of the Boo. With a simple neighborhood listing or a quick amendment to the covenants, we'll never again risk being beaten to the Boo or accidentally Booing a Boo-Humbug. Most importantly, a registry will ensure that you get exactly what you want in your Boo basket.

Sign me up for gin—the good stuff.

Containing My Desire

EVERY GIRL REMEMBERS HER FIRST TIME. THE DAY I LOST MY Container Store virginity I walked around an outdoor shopping mall in north Dallas for forty minutes, wondering if I was really ready.

I had resisted the peer pressure for years, telling myself I didn't need to go all the way, that it was enough to live vicariously through the other girls. Once those doors opened, there was no going back. Just inside the store I pried myself away from magnetic locker organizers designed to hold lip gloss, concealer, and other essentials for surviving high school. Despite the fact that I'm not in high school and have no locker of any kind, I actually had to tell myself—repeatedly—that I had no use for such things. This is how seductive The Container Store can be. I moved on, especially lustful in the office aisle with its designer manila folders and coordinating thumbtacks.

Hurt me.

LELA DAVIDSON

Though I have yearned for drawer dividers in Staples, ached in the closet aisle of Lowes, and gotten hot among the office supplies at Target, nothing compared to my newfound hunger for The Container Store. Walking those mesmerizing rows promising a clutter-free Utopia, it was clear: The Container Store and I had chemistry. I just knew we had potential for a significant union. However, long distance relationships can be tricky and my new lover lived five hours away.

Cue the tear-filled goodbye.

We met online for weeks, each virtual rendezvous igniting the fires of my deep organizational need. You'd think that getting a taste of the real thing would have ruined me for catalogs, home décor magazines and other websites, but after getting together with The Container Store I consumed more home org porn than ever. I inhaled perfect magazine layouts where the meal on the table coordinates with the dishes and the kitchen curtains; where the wardrobe is monochromatic and matches the season.

I crave organization, the way it makes me simplify, forces me to cull all those unnecessary objects from my life—or at least contain them in space-efficient decorative bins. The process isn't just for stuff; it works for ideas too. Just check my hard drive, my internet spaces, and the 3-ring binders that grace my Dewey Decimal worthy bookshelves.

I skipped through my days in slow motion, believing I'd found a soul mate, one who agreed that life is better when its contents are properly stowed and labeled, preferably in a clear typeface.

However, as the weeks passed and no 75% off coupons arrived in the mail, I had to admit that The Container Store wasn't really as into me as I hoped. But I don't regret hooking up. It had to happen, eventually. Now I'm a woman—an organized woman. I liked The Container Store, sure, but it's not like I applied for credit with him. Truth was, my new friend opened up an entire world of order and coordination, but I wasn't sure I wanted to commit to a single system.

I'm in the market for a new lover now. I'm totally cool with set-ups and not picky. But if you know someone, I'd fall hard for the type who knows how alphabetize a girl.

Pretending Prada

Hang around kids a while and you'll hear them playing pretend.

Pretend like I was a princess

Pretend like you were a puppy.

Pretend like we were getting married.

And my personal favorite: Pretend like our parents were dead. But that's another story.

After we watched *The Devil Wears Prada*, my daughter pretended to be Meryl Streep. "Where's my coffee?" she demanded, dumping gloves in my lap. I don't blame her for choosing that part. The devil had better handbags.

Grownups play pretend too. Plastic surgeons help us pretend that our breasts are naturally full and perky, that our stomachs are flat and smooth. We pretend to like other people's children. And quiet as it's kept, most of us, at least once in a while, still pretend to be a Princess. Everyone knows a princess needs props.

I swooned over the invitation to a purse party. Knock-off Dior and Chloe? Cocktails and couture? Hot. Okay, not hot as in stolen, but as it turns out—just as illegal. I pretended not to know that part. My friends met me for a cocktail. Or was it two? Anyway—by the time we made it to the party, the dress-up chest was already half empty.

"Hurry up!" they said. "It's first come, first served."

Louis Vuitton, Chanel, and Coach graced the softly lit living room. I handled a red Dolce & Gabbana, and no sooner had I set it down than someone else nabbed it.

"If you think you might want it," a friend whispered, "you need to hold onto it!"

All around me friends and neighbors held multiple bags on their arms.

"Wine?" someone offered.

I accepted and picked up a crocodile Prada while scoping out black and white Chanels and preppy Kate Spades. I'm not even a label girl. Put me in a room by myself with all those "designer" bags and I'd leave empty handed, but surrounded by the other women, I caved. Good thing they weren't serving Kool-Aid. By the end of the evening I was a proud Prada owner.

The next day when I sobered up and looked at my plastic bag in the cruel morning light, I felt a shopper's hangover coming on. Crooked logo, crappy stitching, and chintzy metal rings on the handle. Worst of all, some paint was already cracked, soon to expose the telltale fraying strings on the handle. Not even twelve hours later. That's how long a hundred dollar game of pretend lasts. Talk about a buzz kill.

I knew my Prada was destined for my daughter's dress-up collection, but I had to enjoy it at least a little. Problem was that I felt funny carrying my faux bag. I know from a distance it is supposed to say I'm chic and successful. But what does it say up close? I'm a fool with a plastic bag and a crooked tin triangle? I'm insecure and need a fake label to feel important? I have entirely too much disposable income, but not enough to buy a real bag?

And then there's the problem of compliments. My first impulse is not so gracious. "You like it? Thanks. It's fake." This response of course defeats the purpose of playing make-believe. Perhaps I should say instead, "Of course you love it, daaahhh-ling. It's Prada, daaahhh-ling." If they persist, wanting to know where I got it, I can respond, "I bought it on the streets of New York."

You can do that same. Never been to New York? That's okay. Pretend like you have.

Stripper 101

I HEARD WE'LL GO HOME WITH BRUISES, BUT I KEEP THIS TO myself as we make our way between the giant fish-netted fiberglass legs straddling the entrance to the Stripper 101 class. Why? This is Vegas, Baby, not the carpool line, and the four of us upstanding women crave as much attention, novelty, and adventure as we can get—without actually cheating on our husbands. Besides, it'll be good exercise. This is why we have donned gym clothes and tennis shoes and carried red patent stilettos through lobbies and shopping malls to a dark corner of the Planet Hollywood hotel.

The forty-dollar ticket price included a drink, which we were encouraged to order before class. However, because we are still recovering from last night's bottle service, we delay the drinking and focus our energy on coming up with stripper names as instructed by the girl who swiped our credit cards. Text message fly as we attempt to include the men back home in our faux-debauchery. Between us we come up with Cherry Pop, Roxy Cock, Misty Storms, Stormy Rains, Candi, Brandi, Peaches, and because I am traveling with Southerners, Dixie McTits.

I settle on Stretchmark.

While we wait, a girl with a camera leads groups of women to a smudged brass pole mounted on a platform in the corner. They make fish lips, lift their chests, and touch each other in front of leopard print wallpaper. When it's our turn I end up kneeling, as I have in every group photograph since I was seven—short girl front and center, fearing panty reveal. Except now I'm grasping a stripper pole.

And no anti-bacterial wipes in sight.

After the pictures we are escorted into the club, past the wall of t shirts with cartoon women in tiny aprons dancing with mops and the slogan "Grab life by the pole." Because clearly it is every woman's dream to have not only sex appeal, but also a killer chicken pot pie and gleaming hardwoods. Be still, my beating Stepford heart.

We are shown into a room at the end of the hall, home to a dozen stripper poles, stacks of chairs, and on two walls, floor to ceiling mirrors. Unlike the light absorbing chalky black of the rest of the club, this room is painted in warm tones, which take the edge off my "daytime in Vegas" look—basically eye cream and a shade of lipstick intended to draw attention away from my less-than-glowing everything else.

Our teacher introduces herself as a *retired* stripper, perfectly delivering the line, "My teenagers have no idea what Mom used to do for a living." Her name is Kindra, with an "i," not to be confused with Playboy Playmate Kendra, with an "e," who lends her celebrity endorsement to the class and the line of personal stripper poles sold next to the t-shirts.

"Who has been to a strip club?" Kindra asks. Everyone raises a hand but two of us, an overweight black woman in a nylon track-suit, and me. My friends are visibly surprised. Really? I've never been to a strip club? I scroll through my mind, searching for a single memory of the sticky, glittery, heroin-laced idea I've gathered from TV and films. Nothing.

"Does Hooters count?"

My friends scoot a centimeter away from me while Kindra explains that because pole dancing does not pay as well as lap dancing, most girls in Vegas don't bother to master the advanced moves, which are quite athletic. She tells us there is even a petition to include pole dancing in the 2016 Olympics, a kind of gymnastics, if you think about it. All I can think of is my daughter: "Mom, Coach says we need the check for my pole dancing costume by Friday!"

After a quick warm up and more reassurance about our sexiness, we learn the basics: the walk, the hip roll, the booty grind, and the general shaking of the jiggly parts. Peppered throughout the dance instruction are tips about the business of stripping. As we learn about everything from getting paid up front to making our quotas I wonder which of the four of us would earn enough to cover her pasties.

It occurs to me that Stripper 101 might be less about equipping novice bachelorettes and housewives with enticing moves and more about recruiting them into the industry. It also occurs to me that this is exactly what would occur to a forty-year-old mother of two who has never actually been to a strip club.

We're rapt as Kindra shares insider information. "When a stripper pulls on her panties, she's asking for money."

Who knew?

We practice a simple routine, but the most valuable thing I learn is how to distract a man by rubbing my breasts with an open hand. Why haven't I learned this before? My mind races with practical applications: difficult interview questions, salary negotiations, and anything at a car dealership.

Finally we get to what we've come for: the pole.

I get into position. I'm ready for this. I'm in shape. I'm sexy. I'm fearless!

However, Kindra's instruction has done little to break the spinning process down into manageable components. I fear not bruises, but broken bones. I want to spin like a porn-soaked firefighter, I do. But I realize that navigating the pole in a graceful manner might take years of practice, years that will propel me further and further from Sexy with every cumulative spin. I watch my friends in the mirror. All of them have been endowed with better natural assets, but all are just as uncoordinated as I am.

Thank God we have spreadsheet skills and fully funded 401k's.

After a few minutes of frustrating practice, Kindra announces there has been a request to see some advanced pole work. She is all leg, spinning, twisting, flipping. If that Olympic thing comes through she's certainly a contender, especially with her grand finale, in which, secured only by her biceps, she hovers and undulates parallel to the pole before finishing in a spectacular inverted spin.

Class is dismissed. There is no VIP pass to the front of the souvenir line. And though the t-shirts are cute, it's difficult to imagine wearing one to the grocery store or during an annual performance review. Even with free shipping, the at-home stripper poles would be an impractical purchase. However, we are nothing if not vain, so we stay in line, hoping that the commemorative portrait flatters.

As we leave the club, moving on to the shopping portion of our weekend, I sip a strawberry margarita from a plastic cup and feel the bruises developing on my shins. What happens in Vegas will stay in Vegas, except for a cheesy picture in a tri-fold keeper that I won't show my daughter.

And those stripper names, which I've programmed into my phone. Carpool will never be the same.

Precious

It was my idea to get the dog. I am the one who traveled to the countryside and handed over the hundred dollars for a darling Italian Greyhound with eyes the color of a good sky. I helped the kids come up with his name. Technically he was our dog. However, from now on, Simon officially belongs to my husband. It happened the last time I took him to the vet, where all I heard was, "precious. "

"Oh, how precious."

"Isn't he precious?"

We are not pet people; we keep forgetting.

There were two cats: Cleo, who sneezed green pus, and Pita, who picked fights with raccoons. Our first dog, Sadie the Schnauzer, bit to draw blood and ate a hole through the laundry room wall. Despite our many pet misfortunes, when my husband started working out of the country I decided I needed a watchdog.

Instead of watching, Simon runs. I should have known this. The word, "Greyhound," should have been a clue. He sleeps on the furniture and demands to be let in and out, and sometimes back in and back out—all at his convenience. We have to feed him every day. As if that weren't enough, he gets sick. Tumors, rashes, bugs in his ear. At the vet's office they fawn over Simon.

He's so gorgeous.

He's so friendly.

He's just *precious*.

No one at the pediatric clinic is ever excited to see my human children. They're treated like the walking Petrie dishes they are. But the dog is precious. In the exam room the vet tech holds Simon in some vet Zen move and takes his temperature rectally. When he steps out to get the doctor, Simon jumps the three feet to the floor.

The tech whips around. "Did he just jump off the table?"

I nod. The tech makes sure Simon is okay before turning his judging eyes on me as if I'd let the baby roll off the changing table.

"Bad dog," I say, trying to demonstrate my parental concern.

The doctor comes in, ignores me and greets Simon with baby talk. She asks me about the rash on his belly and I admit to giving him Benadryl. (I don't admit to taking veterinary advice from my bug lady.) The vet tells me to double the dose.

"We'll wait until the first frost," she says, "If he's still scratching after that we'll look into food allergies."

I don't tell her that when my son was so sick last year, when the doctor couldn't figure out what was wrong, when he lost ten pounds—even then I only briefly considered looking into food allergies. She asks what Simon eats, and I should say dog food. Instead I say, "Purina Beneful—and that gravy looking stuff, the stuff in the packet." I'm doomed either way because the name of his food does not contain the word science or something unpronounceable.

The vet asks if Simon is bathed regularly and I give my first good answer. She likes that we use oatmeal shampoo. We being my husband. The oatmeal was his idea, which is good considering Simon is officially his dog now.

"Are you using anything medicated?" the vet asks.

"No," I say, smiling and overconfident now, "just the overpriced over-the-counter stuff."

She says that's good, but is going to give—and by give she means sell—me some shampoo I'm to use every other week. Every other week. As if I'm going to create a tracking schedule for shampooing the dog. I can't even keep track of the once a month heartworm pills he's supposed to take, the ones advertised by the model on the vet's shelf of the dog-sized heart infested with thin white worms.

In addition to antihistamine for the itching, I'm supposed to give Simon antibiotics for the staph infection brought on by the scratching. The vet assures me this rash isn't contagious to humans. However, the sore on his neck might be—if it's ringworm. We won't know for ten days. In the meantime I need to treat it with anti-fungal ointment. Tinactin, she says.

I'm waiting at the check out counter among things I'll never buy: designer leashes, pet cologne, and a lit candle that claims to mask pet odor. Suddenly a tiny dog poops and the staff spring into action like in those scenes on every medical drama when a gunshot victim is wheeled through the door. The new girl rushes up with a wad of paper towels, but old hands stop her.

"We don't just clean it up. We need to culture it!"

Another itty-bitty dog steps in the runny poop.

Surprisingly, the candle works. I don't smell a thing.

The crisis passes and I get my bill. The exam, skin scraping, fungal culture, Cephalexin, and Benzoyl Plus shampoo comes to $101.64, over five times what I pay for my human child to see a doctor. To the vet's credit, in a couple of days she will call to see how Simon is feeling. Pediatricians don't do that.

On the way home I stop at Walgreen's for the anti-fungal cream. The generic brand is cheaper, but also has a different ingredient and I need to make sure I get the right one because it's not called in-case-your-dog-has-ringworm cream. It's called something else. The young male pharmacist says it's fine. He doesn't buy my dog story. In eighteen years I've never asked my husband to pick up a box of tampons. Now I'm buying jock itch cream for his dog.

Precious.

Words in the Sand

THE FIRST MORNING AT THE BEACH MY DAUGHTER AND I WOKE before everyone else. We stood in awe of the waves, our amazement bonding us in an idyllic instant. No arguments about toast, shouting over sunscreen, or fights for the remote. For a rare moment everything was perfect. I'm greedy for those times. I seek the formula that transforms motherhood into a Kodak moment.

There's no such equation.

The variables of motherhood shift constantly, and are usually at odds. I had a baby to meet some selfish need, only to find that every future choice requires selflessness. Robbed of the libido that created the child in the first place, I've channeled my energy into chopping the broccoli that is spit at me. Everyone depends on me, the woman who cannot remember the word for pancake. I've swelled with irrational pride at the first step, and crumbled under the shame of screaming at a two-year-old.

The grit of motherhood smoothes my rough edges—when I let it. It is a mandate to create order in a world I have no control over. Motherhood is lying to foster hope, and telling the truth because that's all there is. It means knowing children will break my heart when they leave, and not wanting it any other way.

The afternoon waves came faster and harder. My daughter struggled to shape words in the dense wet sand before they disappeared in the tide. I could have helped, but she wouldn't let me. That's the paradox: She doesn't belong to me, but I'm responsible for her.

While nothing about motherhood is constant, there are split seconds where everything is in balance. If we are lucky, we grasp those moments and seal them in our hearts before the waves of life wash them away.

And then we start all over, carving out a new word in the sand.

ACKNOWLEDGEMENTS

〜〰〜

SPECIAL THANKS TO ALL MY FAMILY, AND ESPECIALLY THOSE who read early and awful drafts. Same goes for all my wise girl-friends, without whom I would be lost: Wendy Bailey, Brandi Barnett, Shannon Bieda, Lori Bremer, Wonder Bright, Rebecca Chayni, Kelly Emeterio, Lisa Gray, Catherine Grubbs, Deanna O'Neil, Lydia O'Neill, Bonnie Palasak, Allyson Rhone, Gracie Terrell, Lori Walker and Kim Witt. In addition, I could not have completed this book without the unique support of Diana Calhoun, who knew I could do it; Stephanie Parsley, for that day at Chuck-E-Cheese; Mary Ann Powers, for unceasing inspiration; and Tina Winham, who reminded me how to make it happen.

Special thanks to the Northwest Arkansas Writers Guild: Raymona Anderson, Vic Fountain, Rhonda Franz, Denton Gay, June Jefferson, Marilyn Lanford, Jan Larkcy, Maeve Maddox, Joe Tangari, Pat Prinsloo, Barbara Youree, and especially Marilyn Collins, my publishing mentor. Also, Tim McGinn, who sneaked me into the group without a single clip.

Thanks to Lynn Troung for giving me an online platform for the very first of these essays, and to Kimberly Enderle and *Peekaboo* magazine for first publishing them in print. Thanks to Ron Mattocks for answering emails with the misleading subject line: one quick question, and to all the regional parenting magazine editors who have published these works, especially those who included notes telling me I made them laugh.

Thanks to William Bernhardt for creating events for writers in Tulsa; Barry Friedman for unwavering encouragement without a speck of coddling; and Christina Katz for gentle nudges in the right direction. Thanks to the Oklahoma Writers Federation, Inc. for producing a conference that always exceeds my expectations and that has been integral to my writing education and an inspiration to continue during the long lonely days.

For early support of the completed manuscript, I thank Lisa Quinn, Kelly Wallace, Wendi Aarons, Rita Arens, Kiki Bochi, and Christine Candelaria.

Incredible thanks to my editor, Patricia Smith, for making sure that each and every page produced a smile. And thank you, Nancy Cleary at Wyatt-MacKenzie, for everything else.

About the Author

LELA DAVIDSON is the Managing Editor of ParentingSquad.com and the Associate Editor of *Peekaboo* magazine. Her writing is featured regularly in family and parenting magazines throughout the United States and Canada, and in *Chicken Soup for the Soul: New Moms*.

www.LelaDavidson.com